Diet recommendations for high cholesterol

Please check these recommendations always with a nutrition consultant, therapist, doctor or dietician. The recipes and the list of ingredients are supporting the conventional medical therapy.
The calorie disclosures of fresh ingredients (fruit and vegetables) vary according to quality and time of harvest. The contents were checked by a dietician and a nutrition consultant for the Traditional Chinese Medicine (TCM).

Author:
©2017 Josef Miligui
www.ebns.at

AF285252

Source:
The lists are created from the EBNS database for nutritional counseling. The database is used by dietitians, therapists and doctors for advising the patient / client.

Literature:
The specialist literature and the training documents of the German and Austrian dietary and traditional Chinese medicine serve as a knowledge base. We have used the documents as a basis of knowledge, adapted it to our experience and completed them.
http://di-book.com

Title Photo:
©2008 Erika Weixlbaumer

Production and publishing:
BoD – Books on Demand, Norderstedt
ISBN: 9783752861532

Diet recommendations for DIETETICS - Metabolism - Fat metabolism - hypercholesterolaemia high cholesterol)

1   Treatment strategy 5
2   Avoid 5
3   Breakfast 5
4   Snack 6
5   Lunch 7
6   Afternoon 9
7   Dinner 9
8   Any time 10
9   Recipes 12
    9.1   8 treasures of rice 12
    9.2   Adzuki Bean and Rice Soup 12
    9.3   Apple - banana cream 13
    9.4   Asparagus with lemon pesto 14
    9.5   Barley and vegetable soup 14
    9.6   Barley mash with steamed pear 15
    9.7   Barley soup 16
    9.8   Basic recipe for a beef broth (clear) 16
    9.9   Basic recipe for a chicken broth worming 17
    9.10   Basic recipe for a fish broth 18
    9.11   Basic recipe for a reissue soup (Congee) 19
    9.12   Basic recipe for a vegetable soup, nutritious 19
    9.13   Bean paste piquant sweet 20
    9.14   Beef pumpkin and vegetable stew 21
    9.15   Beef salad 22
    9.16   Beluga lentil stew with vegetables 22
    9.17   Black root with yogurt 23
    9.18   Black-eyed beans stew 24
    9.19   Blueberry puree 24
    9.20   Breakfast - Rice with fruits 25
    9.21   Bulgur with tomatoes and fresh herbs 25
    9.22   Carrot and potato rucola sandwich 26
    9.23   Carrot and rice gruel soup 27
    9.24   Carrot Risotto 27
    9.25   Champignon salad with cress 28
    9.26   Chicken soup with angelica root and buckthorn fruit 29
    9.27   Chicken soup with green spelt, parsley and sake 29
    9.28   Chickpeas with Raisins 30
    9.29   Chicory salad with tangerine 31

9.30	Coconut rice with cardamom	31
9.31	Colorful tuscan bean soup	33
9.32	Compote from apples	33
9.33	Compote from cherries	34
9.34	Corn coffee with cardamom	34
9.35	Cous-Cous with date, coco and almondpuree	35
9.36	Cucumber salad	35
9.37	Cucumber soup	36
9.38	Fast polenta with avocado and spring onion	36
9.39	Fennel with roasted walnuts	37
9.40	Fine Russian borscht	38
9.41	Fish soup with rosemary	39
9.42	Fried asparagus with rocket	39
9.43	Hearty polenta mash	40
9.44	Hummus (Chickpeas mash)	41
9.45	Hungarian rice salad	42
9.46	Italian champignon rice	42
9.47	Japanese algae soup	43
9.48	Kohlrabi in chervil sauce with potatoes	44
9.49	Leek soup with almond mash	45
9.50	Lentils and rice stew	46
9.51	Marinated cod on pumpkin puree	46
9.52	Marinated turkey with cashew nuts from the wok	47
9.53	Melanzani with olive oil and turmeric	48
9.54	Millet with pears	49
9.55	Minestrone	50
9.56	Mung bean stew	51
9.57	Oven potatoes with celery-curd cheese (quark)	51
9.58	Oyster mushrooms with asparagus	52
9.59	Parsley cream sauce	53
9.60	Pear compote	54
9.61	Plum Cake	54
9.62	Polenta with peach	55
9.63	Polenta with ratatouille	56
9.64	Potato with dandelion salad	57
9.65	Potato-basil soup	57
9.66	Potatoes with curd cheese sauce	58
9.67	Potatoes with wild garlic-curd cheese	59
9.68	Pumpkin slices with spicy rice	59
9.69	Pumpkin soup	60
9.70	Quick zucchini soup	61
9.71	Refreshing cucumber soup with potatoes	62
9.72	Rhubarb and apple jelly	62

9.73	Rhubarb cake with sprinkles	63
9.74	Rice congee with carrots and fennel	64
9.75	Rice congee with dried fruit	65
9.76	Rice porridge with shrubs (seeds) Yi Yi Ren	66
9.77	Roasted barley patties	66
9.78	Rosemary Potatoes	67
9.79	Rucola salad with tomatoes	68
9.80	Russian kasha with white cabbage	68
9.81	Salmon on tomato-spinach	69
9.82	Sliced turkey with zucchini	70
9.83	Spelled with fruit and nuts	71
9.84	Spicy avocado cream with cottage cheese	71
9.85	Spicy Tofu Vegetable Pan	72
9.86	Tea Black tea (Russian tea)	73
9.87	Tea from Melissa	74
9.88	Tea Green tea	74
9.89	Tofu-Black Bean Chili with Rice	75
9.90	Tomato soup	76
9.91	Tsampa with jam or fruit compote	76
9.92	Turkey rolls in tomato cream	77
9.93	Vegetable bowl with Provencal pistou	78
9.94	Vegetable juice	79
9.95	Vegetable miso soup with tofu	79
9.96	Vegetable semolina soup	80
9.97	Warming carrot soup	81
9.98	Wheatgrass porridge with pink grapefruit	81
9.99	Whole milk cereal mash	82
10	Effects of food	83
10.1	Use ingredients: recommendable	83
10.2	Use ingredients: yes	83
10.3	Use ingredients: little	89
10.4	Do not use contra-acting foods	90
11	Herbs and their effects	91
11.1	Basil	91
11.2	Dill	91
11.3	Chervil dried	91
11.4	Coriander	91
11.5	Herbs various	91
11.6	Cress	91
11.7	Chives	91
11.8	Lovage	91
11.9	Lily bulbs	92
11.10	Dandelion (young plants)	92

11.11	Balm	92
11.12	Oregano dried	92
11.13	Parsley	92
11.14	Peppermint	92
11.15	Rosemary	92
11.16	Sage	92
11.17	Black caraway	93
11.18	Thyme dried	93
11.19	King Solomon's-seal	93
11.20	Yam root, yam root tuber	93
12	Basics of Nutrition	94
12.1	Nutrition	94
12.2	Recipes	96
12.3	Foodstuffs	96
12.4	Herbs	97
13	Other dietic-books	98

1   Treatment strategy

An increased cholesterol level can be reduced quite easily - you have to "only": remove overweight, replace animal fat with vegetable fats, increase the intake of unsaturated fatty acids (linseed oil, walnut oil, rapeseed oil, thistle oil, olive oil, sea fish).
Put plenty of dietary fiber (potatoes, cereals) in the daily food plan.
Do not drink or drink alcohol (except a 1/8 l red wine per day), do not smoke. Avoid foods with high sugar content. Do not use finished products.

2   Avoid

Fat food with an unfavorable fat-acid pattern, saturated fatty acids like butter, sunflower oil, hot-pressed oils, eggs, entrails.
Caloric foods that inhibit weight reduction.

3   Breakfast

	kkal. per serving
Adzuki Bean and Rice Soup	199
Apple - banana cream	110
Barley mash with steamed pear	113
Bean paste piquant sweet	311

Blueberry puree 10
Breakfast - Rice with fruits.. 230
Bulgur with tomatoes and fresh herbs.. 205
Carrot and potato rucola sandwich 94
Chickpeas with Raisins 429
Coconut rice with cardamom.. 266
Colorful tuscan bean soup.. 249
Compote from apples... 67
Compote from cherries... 31
Corn coffee with cardamom.. 3
Cous-Cous with date, coco and almondpuree............................ 483
Fast polenta with avocado and spring onion 449
Hearty polenta mash... 262
Hummus (Chickpeas mash) 542
Hungarian rice salad 421
Kohlrabi in chervil sauce with potatoes 187
Leek soup with almond mash.. 115
Millet with pears 213
Pear compote 100
Plum Cake... 502
Polenta with peach.. 197
Potato with dandelion salad.. 162
Potato-basil soup 95
Refreshing cucumber soup with potatoes 148
Rhubarb and apple jelly.. 180
Rhubarb cake with sprinkles... 475
Rice congee with dried fruit 210
Rice porridge with shrubs (seeds) Yi Yi Ren............................... 211
Roasted barley patties 398
Spelled with fruit and nuts 289
Spicy avocado cream with cottage cheese 613
Tea Black tea (Russian tea) 7
Tea Green tea... 2
Tsampa with jam or fruit compote... 280
Vegetable miso soup with tofu.. 106

4   Snack

Adzuki Bean and Rice Soup.. 199
Apple - banana cream... 110
Carrot and potato rucola sandwich 94
Hummus (Chickpeas mash) 542
Plum Cake... 502

Polenta with ratatouille 225
Rhubarb cake with sprinkles.. 475
Wheatgrass porridge with pink grapefruit....................... 398

5   Lunch

X8 treasures of rice.. 212
Adzuki Bean and Rice Soup.. 199
Asparagus with lemon pesto 171
Barley and vegetable soup.. 281
Barley mash with steamed pear 113
Barley soup... 265
Bean paste piquant sweet 311
Beef pumpkin and vegetable stew............................... 369
Beef salad... 249
Beluga lentil stew with vegetables 201
Black root with yogurt.. 424
Black-eyed beans stew 140
Blueberry puree 10
Bulgur with tomatoes and fresh herbs.......................... 205
Carrot and potato rucola sandwich 94
Carrot and rice gruel soup... 101
Carrot Risotto.. 308
Champignon salad with cress....................................... 220
Chicken soup with angelica root and buckthorn fruit 77
Chicken soup with green spelt, parsley and sake........... 150
Chickpeas with Raisins 429
Chicory salad with tangerine 256
Coconut rice with cardamom 266
Colorful tuscan bean soup... 249
Compote from apples... 67
Compote from cherries... 31
Corn coffee with cardamom.. 3
Cous-Cous with date, coco and almondpuree................ 483
Cucumber salad... 27
Cucumber soup.. 95
Fast polenta with avocado and spring onion 449
Fennel with roasted walnuts 342
Fine Russian borscht 171
Fish soup with rosemary 271
Fried asparagus with rocket 148
Hearty polenta mash... 262
Hummus (Chickpeas mash) 542

Hungarian rice salad 421
Italian champignon rice 256
Japanese algae soup 47
Kohlrabi in chervil sauce with potatoes 187
Leek soup with almond mash 115
Lentils and rice stew.. 232
Marinated cod on pumpkin puree 201
Marinated turkey with cashew nuts from the wok.................. 318
Melanzani with olive oil and turmeric 432
Millet with pears 213
Minestrone... 210
Mung bean stew... 665
Oven potatoes with celery-curd cheese (quark)..................... 304
Oyster mushrooms with asparagus 316
Parsley cream sauce.. 118
Pear compote 100
Polenta with peach.. 197
Polenta with ratatouille 225
Potato with dandelion salad.. 162
Potato-basil soup 95
Potatoes with curd cheese sauce 413
Potatoes with wild garlic-curd cheese.................................... 254
Pumpkin slices with spicy rice 437
Pumpkin soup.. 104
Quick zucchini soup 41
Refreshing cucumber soup with potatoes 148
Rhubarb and apple jelly... 180
Rice congee with carrots and fennel 131
Rice congee with dried fruit 210
Rice porridge with shrubs (seeds) Yi Yi Ren.......................... 211
Roasted barley patties 398
Rosemary Potatoes.. 188
Rucola salad with tomatoes... 129
Russian kasha with white cabbage.. 250
Salmon on tomato-spinach... 364
Sliced turkey with zucchini.. 281
Spicy avocado cream with cottage cheese 613
Spicy Tofu Vegetable Pan... 241
Tea Black tea (Russian tea) 7
Tea Green tea... 2
Tofu-Black Bean Chili with Rice.. 343
Tomato soup... 100
Turkey rolls in tomato cream 301

Vegetable bowl with Provencal pistou.. 137
Vegetable miso soup with tofu.. 106
Vegetable semolina soup 198
Warming carrot soup... 133

6 Afternoon

Apple - banana cream... 110
Carrot and potato rucola sandwich 94
Fast polenta with avocado and spring onion 449
Hummus (Chickpeas mash) 542
Plum Cake... 502
Rhubarb cake with sprinkles... 475

7 Dinner

Adzuki Bean and Rice Soup.. 199
Asparagus with lemon pesto 171
Barley and vegetable soup 281
Barley soup... 265
Beef pumpkin and vegetable stew... 369
Beef salad.. 249
Beluga lentil stew with vegetables 201
Black root with yogurt... 424
Black-eyed beans stew 140
Blueberry puree 10
Carrot Risotto.. 308
Champignon salad with cress... 220
Chicken soup with angelica root and buckthorn fruit 77
Coconut rice with cardamom.. 266
Compote from apples.. 67
Compote from cherries.. 31
Corn coffee with cardamom.. 3
Cous-Cous with date, coco and almondpuree............................. 483
Fennel with roasted walnuts 342
Fine Russian borscht 171
Fish soup with rosemary 271
Fried asparagus with rocket 148
Hearty polenta mash 262
Hungarian rice salad 421
Japanese algae soup 47
Kohlrabi in chervil sauce with potatoes.. 187
Lentils and rice stew.. 232
Marinated cod on pumpkin puree 201

Marinated turkey with cashew nuts from the wok............................ 318
Melanzani with olive oil and turmeric 432
Millet with pears 213
Minestrone.. 210
Mung bean stew.. 665
Oven potatoes with celery-curd cheese (quark)............................. 304
Parsley cream sauce... 118
Pear compote 100
Polenta with peach.. 197
Polenta with ratatouille 225
Potato with dandelion salad... 162
Potato-basil soup 95
Potatoes with curd cheese sauce 413
Pumpkin slices with spicy rice 437
Pumpkin soup 104
Quick zucchini soup 41
Refreshing cucumber soup with potatoes 148
Rice porridge with shrubs (seeds) Yi Yi Ren.................................. 211
Roasted barley patties 398
Rosemary Potatoes.. 188
Rucola salad with tomatoes... 129
Russian kasha with white cabbage.. 250
Salmon on tomato-spinach.. 364
Sliced turkey with zucchini... 281
Spicy avocado cream with cottage cheese 613
Spicy Tofu Vegetable Pan... 241
Tea Black tea (Russian tea) 7
Tea Green tea.. 2
Tofu-Black Bean Chili with Rice... 343
Tomato soup.. 100
Vegetable bowl with Provencal pistou.. 137
Vegetable miso soup with tofu... 106
Vegetable semolina soup 198
Warming carrot soup.. 133
Wheatgrass porridge with pink grapefruit...................................... 398
Whole milk cereal mash 205

8   Any time

Basic recipe for a reissue soup (Congee) 140
Blueberry puree 10
Carrot and rice gruel soup.. 101
Coconut rice with cardamom.. 266

Compote from apples.. 67
Compote from cherries.. 31
Corn coffee with cardamom... 3
Pear compote 100
Polenta with ratatouille 225
Potato with dandelion salad.. 162
Rice congee with carrots and fennel... 131
Rice porridge with shrubs (seeds) Yi Yi Ren................................... 211
Tea Black tea (Russian tea) 7
Tea Green tea... 2
Whole milk cereal mash 205

9 Recipes

(recommendable) = You can use more.
(little) = You should use less than specified or omit.

9.1 8 treasures of rice

Diuretic, warming the body from the inside, expands blood vessels, strengthens the muscles, regulates internal organs functions, promotes spleen, calms nerves.
Cooking time approx. 1 hour
Calories p. portion: 212
4 portions
Allergens:

Quantity of ingredients:
Lily bulbs 1 table spoon / 5g. (recommended)
Longane 1 table spoon / 5g. (yes)
King Solomon's-seal 1 table spoon / 5g. (yes)
Yam root, yam root tuber 1 table spoon / 5g. (yes)
Coix (seeds) YiYi Ren 1 table spoon / 5g. (yes)
Rice wild (nature rice) 1 1/2 cups / 240g. (recommended)
Water 8-10 cups / 800g. (yes)

Cooking instructions:
Each one 1 tbsp: Bai He, Longan, Yu Zhu, Da Zao, Shan Yao, Lian Mi, Yi Yi Ren, Qian Shi

Add hot water and soak for about 30 minutes. Then add 1 - 2 cups of rice (normal) and simmer for 1/2 to 1 hour until the rice is very soft. Or: Cook for about 3 hours with the herbs a congee. Then the herbs do not have to be soaked.

9.2 Adzuki Bean and Rice Soup

Strengthens spleen, heart, kidney and stomach, supports urination, improves blood circulation, reduces inflammation.
Cooking time approx. 2 hours
Calories p. portion: 199
1 portions
Allergens:

Quantity of ingredients:
Adzuki beans 8 table spoons / 40g. (recommended)
Rice round grain 2 table spoons / 20g. (yes)
Water 1 1/2 cups / 200g. (yes)
Honey 1 table spoon / 8g. (yes)

Cooking instructions:
Boil soaked adzuki beans and round grain rice in a ratio of 4: 1 in water until a thin pulp has formed. Sweet as needed; possibly puree.

Effect: This recipe strengthens kidney, spleen and stomach and is particularly suitable for mothers with too little milk flow.

9.3   Apple - banana cream

Regulates gastrointestinal function, provides vitamin C, cholesterol lowering, reduces inflammation, diuretic, improves blood circulation.
Cooking time approx. 15 min
Calories p. portion: 110
4 portions
Allergens:

Quantity of ingredients:
Apple (sour) 7/8 lbs / 400g. (yes)
Water 3/4 cup - 6 oz / 200g. (yes)
Orange peel 1/4 piece / 5g. (yes)
Lemon peel 1/2 piece / 2g. (yes)
Sugar brown 2 teaspoons / 6g. (little)
Cinnamon sticks 1 piece / 0g. (yes)
Banana 1 piece / 150g. (yes)
Acerola fruit nectar or powder 1 teaspoon / 2g. (recommended)
Orange juice 1/2 piece / 50g. (yes)
Lemon juice 1 table spoon / 10g. (yes)

Cooking instructions:
Cut the apple into fine slices, bring water to boil and add the apple slices, orange- and lemon peel, sugar and cinnamon and simmer about 7 minutes. The apples should be almost soft. Remove acerola and the cinnamon stick.
Mix the apple, the banana, the orange juice and the lemon juice.

9.4   Asparagus with lemon pesto

Diuretic, improves blood circulation, prevents cancer, forcing spleen, promotes weight loss. Good to fight immunodeficiency, loss of appetite, arteriosclerosis, flatulence, bladder weakness, anemia, high blood pressure, depressions, diabetes, diarrhea, vomiting.
Cooking time approx. 20 min
Calories p. portion: 172
2 portions
Allergens: H

Quantity of ingredients:
Asparagus (green or white) 1,1 lbs / 500g. (yes)
Lemon 1 piece / 35g. (yes)
Water hot 1/2 cup / 50g. (yes)
Boxhorn clover seeds 1 pinch / 0,2g. (yes)
Olive oil 2 table spoons / 20g. (yes)
Almond 1 table spoon / 8g. (yes)
Sugar cane sugar 1 pinch / 0,5g. (little)
Garlic 1 clove / 2g. (yes)
Pepper (ground) 1 pinch / 0,2g. (yes)
Salt 1 pinch / 0,5g. (yes)

Cooking instructions:
Peel the asparagus (the whites whole, the greens only at the bottom). Peel and cut diagonally into pieces about 3
cm long. In the steam sieve the white about 12 minutes, the green about 10 minutes to cook. Cut the lemon into
small pieces, remove seeds. Add the remaining ingredients and puree to a creamy sauce. Arrange the asparagus
and cover with the lemon pesto.
This fits rice, bulgur or millet.

9.5   Barley and vegetable soup

Supports urination, detoxifying, promotes spleen and liver, reduces blood pressure, strengthens immune system, prevents cancer, reduces radiation damage, promotes digestion, helps to digest fat, harmonizes metabolism.
Cooking time approx. 2 hours
Calories p. portion: 281
3 portions
Allergens: AGL

Quantity of ingredients:
Barley 1 cup / 120g. (yes)
Shiitake, dried 1/8 oz / 4g. (yes)
Onion (shallot) 1 piece / 20g. (yes)
Cumin (Caraway seed) 1 knife tip / 0,5g. (yes)
Sunflower oil 1 table spoon / 10g. (little)
Water 1 cup / 250g. (yes)
Celery sticks 2 branches / 20g. (yes)
Peas, green 5/8 lbs - 8oz / 250g. (yes)
Tomato 1 piece / 50g. (yes)
Carrot 2 pieces / 150g. (yes)
French beans Handful / 30g. (yes)
Salt 1 pinch / 1g. (yes)
Pepper (ground) 1 pinch / 0,5g. (yes)
Parsley 1 teaspoon / 3g. (yes)
Butter organic 1 teaspoon / 3g. (little)

Cooking instructions:
Soak the barley in the evening for the next day. Soak the mushrooms separately at the next day. Brown onion and cumin in oil, then boil with water. Add the chopped vegetables, some salt, the barley and the shiitake mushrooms and cook everything to a thick soup. At the end, season with pepper, parsley and a little butter.

9.6   Barley mash with steamed pear

Promotes digestion, supports urination, promotes spleen, diuretic, forcing spleen, relaxes, promotes perspiration.
Cooking time approx. 25 min
Calories p. portion: 114
5 portions
Allergens: A

Quantity of ingredients:
Water 10 cups / 1200g. (yes)
Barley 1 cup / 120g. (yes)
Ginger fresh 2 slices / 2g. (yes)
Cardamom 3 capsules / 1g. (yes)
Salt 1 pinch / 1g. (yes)
Pear 1 piece / 200g. (yes)
Sugar cane sugar 1/2 teaspoon / 5g. (little)

Cooking instructions:
Grind coarse the barley and roast it dry. Add hot water, add ginger and cardamom and let it swell to a pulp in low heat. Peel and dice the pear and boil for 10 minutes with a little water. At the end, add the stewed pear, a little butter and sweetener.

Variant: If you want to go fast, you can use barley flakes instead of shot.

9.7   Barley soup

Diuretic, forcing spleen, supports urination, stimulates liver function, antioxidativ, promotes digestion, detoxifying, reduces blood lipids, stimulates, dissolves stagnation.
Cooking time approx. 25 min
Calories p. portion: 265
2 portions
Allergens: A

Quantity of ingredients:
Barley 1 cup / 120g. (yes)
Salt 1 pinch / 1g. (yes)
Ginger fresh 1/2 teaspoon / 1g. (yes)
Olive oil 1 table spoon / 10g. (yes)
Parsley 2 table spoons / 30g. (yes)
Water 1 1/2 cups / 240g. (yes)

Cooking instructions:
Roast the barley in the pan, then grind it to the ground, and boil with water, some salt and ginger to a mash. Before serving add oil and parsley.

Variant: You can add a better taste to the dish if you cook it with prepared vegetable or meat broth.

9.8   Basic recipe for a beef broth (clear)

Strengthens muscles, tendons and bones, reduces blood pressure, strengthens immune system, prevents cancer, reduces radiation damage, stimulates digestion, reduces pain, promotes digestion, diuretic. Rosemary stimulates digestion.
Cooking time approx. 4-8 hours
Calories p. portion: 114
10 portions
Allergens: O

Quantity of ingredients:
Beef soup meat 1,1 lbs / 500g. (little)
Beef meatbones 5/8 oz / 200g. (yes)
Vinegar (Red wine vinegar) 1 dash / 3g. (yes)
Juniper berry 8 pieces / 6g. (yes)
Rosemary 1 pinch / 1g. (yes)
Carrot 3 pieces / 210g. (yes)
Parsnip 2 pieces / 300g. (yes)
Leek 1 piece / 200g. (yes)
Ginger fresh 1/2 teaspoon / 5g. (yes)
Lovage 1 stem / 15g. (yes)
Clove 2 pieces / 2g. (yes)
Pimento 6 pieces / 12g. (yes)
Anise (Common Fennel) 2 pieces / 1g. (yes)
Salt 1 teaspoon / 5g. (yes)
Water 3,3 lbs / 1300g. (yes)

Cooking instructions:
Heat water, a dash of red wine vinegar, some juniper berries, a little rosemary, bones and meat till it boils; add carrot, parsnip, leek, ginger, lovage, clove, allspice, star anise and a little salt; simmer for 4-8 hours then strain.
Refrigerate for later use.

9.9   Basic recipe for a chicken broth worming

Strengthens blood, strengthens bone marrow, reduces blood pressure, strengthens immune system, prevents cancer, reduces radiation damage, promotes sweating, dissolves stagnation, good to fight loss of appetite, flatulence.
Cooking time approx. 2-3 hours
Calories p. portion: 90
9 portions
Allergens: L

Quantity of ingredients:
Chicken meat 1/2 piece / 600g. (yes)
Carrot 2 pieces / 150g. (yes)
Leek 1 stick / 45g. (yes)
Celery root 1 piece / 500g. (yes)
Ginger fresh 2 slices / 2g. (yes)
Fenugreek (Trigonella foenum-graecum) 1 teaspoon / 2g. (yes)

Juniper berry 1 teaspoon / 3g. (yes)
Bay leaf 3 pieces / 2g. (yes)
Water 4 cup / 900g. (yes)

Cooking instructions:
Remove chicken parts from fat. Place chicken pieces in a saucepan
with hot water and heat till it boils briefly, skimming any resulting foam.
Add coarsely chopped vegetables and all spices and cook over medium
heat for 2 to 3 hours. Strain the finished soup. Throw away vegetables
and bones.
Tip: If you want to use the meat as a soup insert, take out after 45
minutes and return only the bones in the soup.
Refrigerate for later use.

9.10 Basic recipe for a fish broth

Strengthens the kidneys, promotes watering, reduces blood pressure,
strengthens immune system, prevents cancer, reduces radiation
damage. Low in cholesterol and protein rich. Improves blood circulation,
stimulates appetite.
Cooking time approx. 40 min
Calories p. portion: 128
5 portions
Allergens: DLO

Quantity of ingredients:
Fish pieces mixed (fresh water) 3/4 lbs / 300g. (recommended)
Celery root 1/4 lbs - 4oz / 120g. (yes)
Leek 2 inches / 10g. (yes)
Carrot 2 pieces / 150g. (yes)
White wine 1/2 cup / 125g. (little)
Lemon 1/2 piece / 50g. (yes)
Bay leaf 2 leaves / 2g. (yes)
Peppercorns 3 pieces / 2g. (yes)
Olive oil 1 table spoon / 10g. (yes)
Water 2 cup / 450g. (yes)

Cooking instructions:
Fry celery, chopped carrots and leeks in olive oil, add bay leaf and
peppercorns, add pieces of fish and sauté briefly. Add water, add little
white wine or lemon. Simmer gently for 30 minutes. Skim off the
resulting foam several times. In the end, sift the ingredients through a
cloth. Refrigerate for later use

9.11 Basic recipe for a reissue soup (Congee)

Low fat content, for the drainage of the body overweight and high blood pressure.
Cooking time approx. 2-4 hours
Calories p. portion: 140
3 portions
Allergens:

Quantity of ingredients:
Rice variety any 1 cup / 120g. (yes)
Water 6 cups / 700g. (yes)

Cooking instructions:
Cook rice and water in a ratio of about 1: 6. The amount of water determines the thickness of the mash (matter of taste).
Put the rice in a saucepan with a heavy lid. It is important to simmer the rice after a short boil on the slightest flame, otherwise it burns.
Boil the rice for 2-4 hours. The longer he cooks, the more he strengthens.
If you want to eat the dish for breakfast, you can put the rice on just before bedtime.
To be on the safe side, you should first check the behavior of your pot and cooker under observation for a similar amount of time, so that nothing burns.
Refrigerate for later use.

9.12 Basic recipe for a vegetable soup, nutritious

Reduces blood pressure, strengthens immune system, prevents cancer, forcing spleen, dissolves stagnation, promotes weight loss. Good to fight immunodeficiency, high blood pressure, depressions, diabetes, diarrhea, reduces blood lipids.
Cooking time approx. 2-3 hours
Calories p. portion: 48
5 portions
Allergens: L

Quantity of ingredients:
Olive oil 1 table spoon / 4g. (yes)
Onion white 1 piece / 60g. (yes)
Carrot 3 pieces / 200g. (yes)
Parsnip 3/8 lbs - 6oz / 150g. (yes)
Celery root 1 cup / 100g. (yes)

Ginger fresh 1/2 teaspoon / 2g. (yes)
Lemon 1/2 piece / 25g. (yes)
Juniper berry 6 pieces / 6g. (yes)
Thyme dried 1 pinch / 1g. (yes)
Lovage 1 table spoon / 3g. (yes)
Bay leaf 2 leaves / 1g. (yes)
Salt 1 pinch / 1g. (yes)
Water 3 cups / 650g. (yes)

Cooking instructions:
Cut the vegetables into cubes.
Heat oil in hot pot, fry shortly onions and vegetables.
Add cold water, then add ginger, bay leaf and lemon juice.
Season with juniper, thyme and lovage. Cover for 2 - 3 hours on a low heat and simmer.
The used vegetables should be thrown away.
The basic recipe serves as a soup base and to refine vegetables, legumes or cereals.
If you want to eat vegetable soup immediately, add the desired vegetables half an hour before. Refrigerate for later use.

9.13 Bean paste piquant sweet

Supports urination, lowers cholesterol, prevents arteriosclerosis, antioxidativ. Promotes digestion, helps to digest fat, supports urination, reduces blood pressure.
Cooking time approx. 1 hour
Calories p. portion: 311
1 portions
Allergens: MO

Quantity of ingredients:
Black beans 1 cup / 120g. (yes)
Ginger fresh 1 inch / 3g. (yes)
Boxhorn clover seeds 1/2 teaspoon / 2g. (yes)
Tomato paste 1 table spoon / 10g. (yes)
Olive oil 2 table spoons / 20g. (yes)
Pumpkin seed oil 1 dash / 3g. (yes)
Mustard 1 knife tip / 1g. (yes)
Radish horseradish 1 teaspoon (grated) / 2g. (yes)
Pepper (ground) 1 pinch / 0,5g. (yes)
Garlic 2 cloves / 3g. (yes)
Salt 1 pinch / 1g. (yes)

Sugar molasses 2 table spoons / 20g. (little)
Lemon peel 1/2 piece / 1g. (yes)

Cooking instructions:
Boil beans (with spices and ginger), drain water and puree. Season with spices.
Refine with sugar beet syrup and lemon peel.

9.14 Beef pumpkin and vegetable stew

Reduces inflammation, improves digestion, reduces blood glucose, strengthens the muscles, tendons and bones, promotes digestion, helps to digest fat.
Cooking time approx. 1 hour
Calories p. portion: 369
4 portions
Allergens: AL

Quantity of ingredients:
Beef meat 3/4 lbs / 350g. (yes)
Pumpkin 3/4 lbs / 350g. (yes)
Leek 3/8 lbs - 6oz / 150g. (yes)
Potato 3/4 lbs / 350g. (yes)
Tomato 3/8 lbs - 6oz / 150g. (yes)
Olive oil 2 table spoons / 25g. (yes)
Basic recipe for a vegetable soup 1/4 lbs - 4oz / 125g. (yes)
Salt 1 pinch / 1g. (yes)
Pepper (ground) 1 pinch / 0,5g. (yes)
Peppers powder 1 teaspoon / 2g. (yes)
Ground caraway 1 pinch / 1g. (yes)
Sugar cane sugar 1 pinch / 1g. (little)
Parsley 1/2 bunch / 30g. (yes)
White bread (wheat bread) 4 slices / 80g. (little)

Cooking instructions:
Dice beef. Peel pumpkin and dice. Cut the leek into rings and dice the peeled potatoes.
Brew the tomatoes with boiling water, peel off the skin and dice.
Steam the meat in olive oil and fill with vegetable stock. Add the cleaned vegetables. Season with salt, pepper, paprika, cumin and fructose.
Stew for 30 minutes over low heat.
Season again and sprinkle with parsley and serve with white bread.

9.15 Beef salad

Strengths spleen and stomach, strengthens blood, strengthens the muscles, tendons and bones, diuretic, detoxifying, suppresses conversion of sugar into fat, lowers cholesterol, dissolves stagnation.
Cooking time approx. 10 min
Calories p. portion: 249
1 portions
Allergens: O

Quantity of ingredients:
Beef meat 1/8 lbs - 2oz / 50g. (yes)
Onion white 1/2 oz / 20g. (yes)
Peppers 1 oz / 30g. (yes)
Cucumber (spicy cucumber) 1 oz / 30g. (yes)
Vinegar (Apple vinegar) 2 teaspoons / 5g. (yes)
Rapeseed oil 2 teaspoons / 5g. (yes)
Salt 1 pinch / 0,5g. (yes)
Pepper (ground) 1 pinch / 0,1g. (yes)
Chives 1 table spoon / 7g. (yes)
Bread with carob kernel flour 2 slices / 50g. (yes)

Cooking instructions:
Cook the meat with the basic recipe of a beef broth and let it cool down. Cut into 1 cm slices. Cut the onions into rings, pepper and gherkin into small cubes. Mix all ingredients.
Make the salad marinade with vinegar, oil and salt and pour over, season to taste and strain.

9.16 Beluga lentil stew with vegetables

Promotes sweating, dissolves stagnation. Relieves constipation, strengthens mother milk production, stimulates nerves, detoxifying, reduces inflammation, improves blood circulation. Strengthens heart and kidney, diuretic, calms the stomach, promotes digestion.
Cooking time approx. 20 min
Calories p. portion: 201
5 portions
Allergens:

Quantity of ingredients:
Lentils 1 1/2 cups / 240g. (recommended)
Water 4-5 cups / 500g. (yes)
Carrot 3 pieces / 150g. (yes)

Leek 1 piece / 300g. (yes)
Kohlrabi 1/2 piece / 200g. (recommended)
Tomato 2 pieces / 80g. (yes)
Onion white 1 piece / 50g. (yes)
Bay leaf 2 leaves / 1g. (yes)
Fennel 1 piece / 250g. (yes)
Star anise 2 pieces / 1g. (yes)
Juniper berry 6 pieces / 2g. (yes)
Olive oil 2 table spoons / 30g. (yes)
Salt 1 pinch / 1g. (yes)
Ginger fresh 1/2 teaspoon / 2g. (yes)
Black caraway 1 pinch / 1g. (yes)

Cooking instructions:
Heat oil in hot pot. Fry onions and add diced vegetables and spices, lentils (washed well) and salt. Cover with cold water (3 fingers wide) and cook for 20 minutes on a low heat.
Sprinkle with fresh herbs and black cumin. Goes well with rice!

9.17 Black root with yogurt

Stimulates kidney, bladder and forces the cleaning of the body. In the physiological sense, they generally stimulate the glands in the organism. Good to fight acute or chronic constipation of the intestine. Rich in Vitamins and trace elements.
Cooking time approx. 20 min
Calories p. portion: 424
2 portions
Allergens: AG

Quantity of ingredients:
Salsify 1 lbs / 400g. (yes)
Yogurt (natural, 1.5% fat) 4 table spoons / 80g. (yes)
Herbs various 1 table spoon / 8g. (yes)
Salt 1 pinch / 1g. (yes)
Herbs various 2 table spoons / 6g. (yes)
Multi-grain bread (gray bread) 6 slices / 120g. (yes)

Cooking instructions:
Peel the salsify and simmer in salted water until tender. Pour away the water, cool the salsify and cut it to size.
Cover with yoghurt and sprinkle with fresh herbs. Serve with the bread. You can also use the salsify from the conserve.

9.18 Black-eyed beans stew

Strengths spleen and stomach, strengthens the muscles. Supports urination, lowers cholesterol, prevents arteriosclerosis.
Cooking time approx. 20 min
Calories p. portion: 140
5 portions
Allergens:

Quantity of ingredients:
Black-eyed peas 1 cup / 100g. (yes)
Rice variety any 1 1/2 cups / 200g. (yes)
Water 10 cups / 1000g. (yes)

Cooking instructions:
Soak the beans overnight and strain.

In a ratio of 1: 2, simmer the beans together with the rice in the Water. Depending on how hot the flame is and how thin the dish should be, more water must be added.

Variation: Add vegetables fried in oil, such as carrots, celery tubers, onions or leeks.

9.19 Blueberry puree

Bilberry is laxative. Clove dissolves stagnation. Cinnamon powder heats stomach and spleen, improves blood circulation.
Cooking time approx. 10 min
Calories p. portion: 10
1 portions
Allergens:

Quantity of ingredients:
Blueberry 1/2 oz / 20g. (yes)
Cinnamon ground 1 pinch / 0,1g. (yes)
Clove 1 piece / 1g. (yes)
Water 1 cup / 250g. (yes)

Cooking instructions:
Boil blueberries with cinnamon and clove in water for 10 minutes. Remove the cinnamon and clove. Puree. Sweet as desired.

9.20 Breakfast - Rice with fruits

Good to fight blood circulation disorders, thrombose, risk of embolism, high blood pressure, a headache, heart attack and stroke. Encourages blood build-up, promotes digestion, reduces Inflammation.
Cooking time approx. 10 min - 3 hours
Calories p. portion: 231
3 portions
Allergens: GHO

Quantity of ingredients:
Basic recipe for a rice soup (Congee) 6 cups / 500g. (yes)
Cow's milk (whole milk 3.5% fat) 1/2 to 1 cup / 80g. (little)
Honey 1 table spoon / 10g. (yes)
Butter organic 1 table spoon / 15g. (little)
Dates dried 1 table spoon / 15g. (yes)
Fig 1 table spoon / 15g. (yes)
Apple (sour) 1 piece / 200g. (yes)
Hazelnuts 1/2 teaspoon / 5g. (yes)
Almond 1/2 teaspoon / 5g. (yes)
Cinnamon ground 1 pinch / 1g. (yes)

Cooking instructions:
Cook rice congee according to basic recipe or use pre-cooked.
Make it with the milk more fluid and sweet with honey.
Fry the fruits and nuts in butter and mix with the finished rice soup, add chopped dates, figs and the apple.

9.21 Bulgur with tomatoes and fresh herbs

Promotes digestion, helps to digest fat, supports urination, reduces blood pressure. Stimulates digestion, supports urination.
Cooking time approx. 30 min
Calories p. portion: 205
1 portions
Allergens: A

Quantity of ingredients:
Bulgur (cereals) 1 cup / 120g. (yes)
Tomato 2 pieces / 70g. (yes)
Rucola 2 table spoons / 16g. (yes)
Pepper powder (hot) 1 pinch / 2g. (yes)
Olive oil 2 table spoons / 20g. (yes)
Pepper (ground) 1 pinch / 0,5g. (yes)

Salt 1 pinch / 1g. (yes)
Basil 4 leaves / 2g. (yes)
Thyme 1 Twig / 3g. (yes)
Lemon juice 1/2 piece / 10g. (yes)

Cooking instructions:
Put cold water in a pot, sprinkle in Bulgur and simmer. Stir in chopped tomatoes, fresh herbs like basil, thyme, arugula, a pinch of rose paprika, lemon juice, a dash of olive oil, a little ground pepper, some salt.
Variant: add some mozzarella.
Recommendation: ideal morning meal in summer; also suitable as evening meal, especially for sleep disorders.

9.22 Carrot and potato rucola sandwich

Reduces inflammation, improves digestion, supports urination, lowers cholesterol, strengthens immune system, prevents cancer, good to fight constipation (Fibre-rich), dissolves stagnation.
Cooking time approx. 20 min
Calories p. portion: 94
4 portions
Allergens: AG

Quantity of ingredients:
Potato (mealy) 5/8 oz / 200g. (yes)
Carrot 1 piece / 50g. (yes)
Sour cream 15% fat 2 table spoons / 45g. (little)
Onion (spring onion) 1 piece / 20g. (yes)
Rucola 1/2 bunch / 100g. (yes)
Lemon peel 1/4 teaspoon / 1g. (yes)
Salt 1 pinch / 1g. (yes)
Pepper (ground) 1 pinch / 0,2g. (yes)
Whole grain bread 8 slices / 48g. (yes)

Cooking instructions:
Cook the potatoes gently, peel and squeeze through the potato press. Cook vegetable broth according to the basic recipe and remove a carrot after a short cooking time and finely crush with a fork.
Stir the potatoes, carrots, grated lemon zest and sour cream into a smooth cream. Mix carrot and potato cream with finely chopped rocket salad. Season the spread with salt and pepper and spread the bread. Sprinkle with the finely chopped young onions.

9.23 Carrot and rice gruel soup

Stops diarrhea, good to fight fever, strengthens immune system, reduces blood pressure.
Cooking time approx. 10 min
Calories p. portion: 101
1 portions
Allergens:

Quantity of ingredients:
Basic recipe for a rice soup (Congee) 1 cup / 120g. (yes)
Carrot 2 pieces / 100g. (yes)
Salt 1 teaspoon / 4g. (yes)

Cooking instructions:
Peel and grate carrots. Heat the rice soup (according to the basic recipe) till it boils and add the grated carrots and salt. Cook for 10 minutes.

9.24 Carrot Risotto

Strengthens immune system, prevents cancer, loss of appetite, flatulence, high blood pressure, depressions, diabetes, diarrhea, stimulates liver function, dissolves stagnation.
Cooking time approx. 45 min
Calories p. portion: 308
2 portions
Allergens: GL

Quantity of ingredients:
Olive oil 1/2 teaspoon / 5g. (yes)
Onion (spring onion) 2 table spoons / 7g. (yes)
Nutmeg 1 pinch / 0,3g. (yes)
Parsley 1/2 bunch / 25g. (yes)
Rice variety any 1/4 lbs - 4oz / 100g. (yes)
Carrot 5/8 lbs - 8oz / 250g. (yes)
Basic recipe for a vegetable soup (nutritious) 1 cup / 280g. (yes)
Fennel seeds ground 1/4 teaspoon / 1g. (yes)
Basil (fresh) 1/2 teaspoon / 2g. (yes)
Salt 1 pinch / 1g. (yes)
Pepper (ground) 1 pinch / 0,3g. (yes)
Parmesan 1 table spoon / 10g. (little)

Cooking instructions:
Heat the oil in a pan, fry the onions in a glassy and very soft manner. Add parsley, sauté briefly. Add rice, carrots and nutmeg, sauté briefly while stirring. Add the vegetable stock, season with fennel and basil, heat till it boils and cook for about 20 minutes until the rice and carrots are well. Stir from time to time and add some vegetable stock if necessary. The risotto should be slightly soupy. Just before the end of the cooking time mix in the white wine and simmer the risotto for a short while. Remove risotto from the heat, mix in Parmesan.

9.25 Champignon salad with cress

Promotes digestion and is good to fight high blood pressure. Good to fight loss of appetite, improves blood circulation.
Cooking time approx. 5 min
Calories p. portion: 220
1 portions
Allergens: AN

Quantity of ingredients:
Champignon 5/8 lbs - 8oz / 250g. (yes)
Sesame oil 2 table spoons / 6g. (yes)
Pepper (ground) 1 pinch / 0,5g. (yes)
Salt 1 pinch / 1g. (yes)
Lemon 1/2 piece / 15g. (yes)
Peppers powder 2 pinches / 0,1g. (yes)
Cress 2 table spoons / 10g. (yes)
White bread (wheat bread) 2 slices / 30g. (little)

Cooking instructions:
Cut mushrooms into thin slices.
Dressing: sesame oil, a little ground pepper, salt, plenty of lemon juice, stir well the rose pepper; give over the finely chopped mushrooms; plenty of watercress.
Goes well with: white bread, round grain rice or quinoa; Along with the cereal, the salad makes a simple, light meal.
Serve with white bread.

9.26 Chicken soup with angelica root and buckthorn fruit

Strengthens bone marrow, reduces blood pressure and blood glucose levels, strengthens immune system, prevents cancer, reduces radiation damage, promotes sweating, dissolves stagnation, affects anorexia, good to fight flatulence.
Cooking time approx. 1 1/2 hours
Calories p. portion: 77
3 portions
Allergens: LO

Quantity of ingredients:
Basic recipe for a chicken soup (warming) 2 cup / 500g. (yes)
Angelica root 1/8 oz / 5g. (yes)
Bocksdorn fruits (Fructus Lycii, Goji, goji berry dried 1/8 lbs - 2oz / 50g. (yes)

Cooking instructions:
When you cook chicken broth according to basic recipes add angelica root and Bocksdorn fruits in the last 40 minutes.
Ingestion: Drink 2-3 cups of broth daily.

9.27 Chicken soup with green spelt, parsley and sake

Strengthens blood, strengthens bone marrow, reduces blood pressure, strengthens immune system, stimulates liver function, detoxifying. Improves blood circulation, improves medication effect, stimulates appetite.
Cooking time approx. 1 1/2 hours
Calories p. portion: 150
2 portions
Allergens: AL

Quantity of ingredients:
Basic recipe for a chicken soup (warming) 2 cup / 500g. (yes)
Green spelt 4 table spoons / 30g. (yes)
Parsley 2 table spoons / 14g. (yes)
Sake 1 dash / 2g. (yes)

Cooking instructions:
Cook the chicken broth according to the basic recipe. Add the ingredients in the soup and simmer 10 min.

9.28 Chickpeas with Raisins

Reduces blood pressure, strengthens immune system. Relaxes breast pressure, moisturizer dry skin, helps to fight incontinence. Strengthens spleen and stomach, strengthens the muscles.
Cooking time approx. 45 min
Calories p. portion: 429
2 portions
Allergens: EGO

Quantity of ingredients:
Chickpeas 1 cup / 120g. (yes)
Hijiki 1 table spoon / 7g. (yes)
Salt 1 pinch / 0,5g. (yes)
Sunflower oil 1 table spoon / 10g. (little)
Carrot 2 pieces / 160g. (yes)
Raisins 2 table spoons / 18g. (yes)
Ginger fresh 1/2 teaspoon / 2g. (yes)
Cumin (Caraway seed) 1 pinch / 0,2g. (yes)
Lemon juice 1 dash / 1g. (yes)
Sour cream 15% fat 1 table spoon / 8g. (little)
Curcuma 1 pinch / 0,2g. (yes)
Soybean milk 1 dash / 1g. (yes)
Coriander 1 pinch / 0,2g. (yes)
Soy sauce 1 dash / 1g. (yes)
Rice round grain 1/2 cup / 60g. (yes)
Water 3 cups / 250g. (yes)
Salt 1 pinch / 1g. (yes)

Cooking instructions:
Preparation:
Soak chickpeas in cold water for several hours or overnight.

After that:
Pour soaking water away; put the chickpeas in cold water; Add 1 tbsp Hijiki and cook the chickpeas bite-proof;
Add salt at the end of the cooking time.

Separately:
In a hot pan, fry oil, chopped carrots (more than chickpeas), raisins, grated ginger, plenty of cumin and salt until the carrots are half cooked; add the chickpeas and sea algae; Add lemon juice, a little sour cream, turmeric, soy or rice milk; a pinch of cilantro, add some soy sauce; Let it

soak for a few minutes over low heat until the carrots are cooked. Put the round grain rice with the water, salt and cook for about 20 minutes.

9.29 Chicory salad with tangerine

Dissolves mucus, is rich in A-B-C Vitamins, promotes digestion, forcing spleen, promotes weight loss. Good to fight loss of appetite, flatulence, immunodeficiency.
Cooking time approx. 10 min
Calories p. portion: 257
3 portions
Allergens: AGNO

Quantity of ingredients:
Tangerine 4 pieces / 300g. (yes)
Chicory 2-3 pieces / 300g. (yes)
Sesame oil 2 table spoons / 18g. (yes)
Pepper (ground) 1 pinch / 0,5g. (yes)
Salt 1 pinch / 1g. (yes)
Vinegar Aceto Balsamico 2 teaspoons / 6g. (yes)
Lemon 1/2 piece / 25g. (yes)
Orange 1/2 piece / 70g. (yes)
Peppers powder 1 pinch / 1g. (yes)
Orange jam 1 teaspoon / 4g. (yes)
Cream, sweet 30% 1 table spoon / 10g. (little)
White bread (wheat bread) 6 slices / 120g. (little)

Cooking instructions:
Peel tangerines and cut into bite-sized pieces; Cut chicory roughly and mix well.
Dressing: sesame oil, pepper, salt, raspberry vinegar or balsamic vinegar, a little lemon or orange juice, rose paprika, orange marmalade or, alternatively, another jam, stir well. Give a little sweet cream over the salad and let it pass briefly.

9.30 Coconut rice with cardamom

Nourishing and slightly warming. Diuretic, reduces blood glucose. Stimulates liver function, detoxifying. Good to fight depressions.
Cooking time approx. 45 min
Calories p. portion: 266
4 portions
Allergens: GO

Quantity of ingredients:
Rice long grain rice 1 cup / 120g. (yes)
Water 6 cups / 400g. (yes)
Sugar cane sugar 1 table spoon / 10g. (little)
Cardamom 1 teaspoon / 2g. (yes)
Ginger fresh 1/2 teaspoon / 2g. (yes)
Butter organic 2 table spoons / 20g. (little)
Coconut grated 2 table spoons / 16g. (yes)
Cashews 1 table spoon / 8g. (yes)
Raisins 1 table spoon / 8g. (yes)
Salt 1 pinch / 0,5g. (yes)
Lemon 1/2 piece / 15g. (yes)
Pumpkin 3/4 lbs / 300g. (yes)
Olive oil 2 table spoons / 20g. (yes)
Coriander 1 pinch / 0,2g. (yes)
Pepper (ground) 1 pinch / 0,2g. (yes)
Curry 1 pinch / 0,5g. (yes)
Water 1/4 cup / 50g. (yes)
Salt 1 pinch / 0,5g. (yes)
Parsley 1 table spoon / 8g. (yes)
Cardamom 1 pinch / 0,2g. (yes)
Turmeric (yellow root) 1 pinch / 0,2g. (yes)

Cooking instructions:
Preparation: Soak long grain rice in cold water for 1 hour and drain.

Then: Heat fresh water till it boils; add some whole cane sugar, plenty of ground cardamom or some cardamom pods, grated ginger and the rice into the hot water and cook.

Separately: heat some butter in a hot pot; add grated coconut, cashews and raisins; add the cooked rice and salt; pour lemon juice over it; mix everything and let it pass for a few minutes.

Pumpkin vegetables: heat olive oil in a pan. Steam the pumpkin (cut in cubes), season with cilantro, pepper and curry, simmer with a little water, salt with sea salt, add chopped parsley with cardamom and turmeric, simmer on a small fire for about 10 minutes, depending on the pumpkin, the pumpkin should still be firm.

9.31 Colorful tuscan bean soup

Promotes digestion, helps to digest fat, supports urination, reduces blood pressure, diuretic, calms the stomach.
Cooking time approx. 2 hours
Calories p. portion: 249
3 portions
Allergens: L

Quantity of ingredients:
Kidney beans (red) 1/8 lbs - 2oz / 50g. (yes)
Chickpeas 1 oz / 25g. (yes)
Lentils 1 oz / 25g. (recommended)
Celery sticks 1 stick / 10g. (yes)
Tomato 2 pieces / 100g. (yes)
Fennel seeds ground 1/2 teaspoon / 1g. (yes)
Salt 1 pinch / 1g. (yes)
Pepper (ground) 1 pinch / 0,5g. (yes)
Garlic 1 clove / 3g. (yes)
Olive oil 2 table spoons / 50g. (yes)
Water 2 1/4 cups / 500g. (yes)
Basil (fresh) 5-7 leaves / 3g. (yes)

Cooking instructions:
Soak legumes, boil and puree. Add vegetables, spices, herbs and oil and cook gently for 2 hours.

Variation: Sweet chestnuts give the dish a special Italian touch.

9.32 Compote from apples

Apple (sweet) stops diarrhea, promotes digestion, appetizing, harmonizes the stomach. Warms stomach and spleen, improves blood circulation.
Cooking time approx. 10 min
Calories p. portion: 67
2 portions
Allergens:

Quantity of ingredients:
Apple (sweet) 1 piece / 220g. (yes)
Water 1 1/2 cups / 220g. (yes)
Cinnamon ground 1 pinch / 1g. (yes)

Cooking instructions:
Cook the apples (organic) with the skin and seeds. Sprinkle with cinnamon.

9.33 Compote from cherries

Improves blood circulation, reduces inflammation, moisturizer dry skin. Warms stomach and spleen.
Cooking time approx. 10 min
Calories p. portion: 32
2 portions
Allergens:

Quantity of ingredients:
Cherry 1/4 lbs - 4oz / 100g. (yes)
Water 1 1/2 cups / 240g. (yes)
Cinnamon ground 1 pinch / 0,2g. (yes)

Cooking instructions:
Cook the cherries in the water until soft. Sprinkle with a little cinnamon.

9.34 Corn coffee with cardamom

Diuretic, forcing spleen, supports urination, relaxes, reduces fat.
Cooking time approx. 5 min
Calories p. portion: 3
1 portions
Allergens:

Quantity of ingredients:
Cereal coffee 1 table spoon / 15g. (yes)
Cardamom 2 cores / 1g. (yes)
Water 1 cup / 120g. (yes)

Cooking instructions:
Boil water, coffee, sugar and cardamom. Let it set for one min before drinking.

9.35 Cous-Cous with date, coco and almondpuree

Stops diarrhea, promotes digestion, appetizing, relieves diarrhea.
Cooking time approx. 10 min
Calories p. portion: 484
3 portions
Allergens: AHO

Quantity of ingredients:
Couscous 1 1/2 cups / 240g. (yes)
Water 4 cups / 400g. (yes)
Dates dried 6 pieces / 20g. (yes)
Coconut flakes 2 table spoons / 30g. (yes)
Almond puree 2 table spoons / 20g. (yes)
Olive oil 2 teaspoons / 20g. (yes)
Apple (sweet) 1 piece grated / 120g. (yes)
Vanilla 1 knife tip / 0,2g. (yes)

Cooking instructions:
Put couscous and olive oil in a large bowl and pour boiling water over
them. Let it swell for 10 minutes. Crush dates and grate apple. Loosen
up cous-cous with a fork. Mix in dates, coconut flakes, apple and
almond paste.
Sweet to taste. Spices and flavors: vanilla, little chili

Winter variation: pear,
Summer variation: apricot, nectarine

9.36 Cucumber salad

Diuretic, detoxifying, suppresses conversion of sugar into fat, lowers
cholesterol, prevents cancer. Cucumber cools and moistens. Dill works
against flatulence, anticonvulsant in gastrointestinal discomfort.
Cooking time approx. 5 min
Calories p. portion: 27
2 portions
Allergens: O

Quantity of ingredients:
Cucumber 1 piece / 400g. (yes)
Salt 1 pinch / 1g. (yes)
Dill 1 pinch / 1g. (yes)
Vinegar (Apple vinegar) 1 table spoon / 10g. (yes)

Cooking instructions:
Cut the cucumber (do not peel the BIO) thinly and season.

9.37 Cucumber soup

Diuretic, detoxifying, suppresses conversion of sugar into fat, lowers cholesterol, prevents cancer, promotes digestion, diaphoretic, dries out, good to fight yeast infections.
Cooking time approx. 20 min
Calories p. portion: 96
4 portions
Allergens: M

Quantity of ingredients:
Olive oil 2 table spoons / 35g. (yes)
Cucumber 2 pieces / 400g. (yes)
Water 2 cup / 500g. (yes)
Sage 3 leaves / 3g. (yes)
Mustard 1/2 teaspoon / 0,5g. (yes)
Coriander 1 pinch / 1g. (yes)
Cardamom 1 pinch / 1g. (yes)
Salt 1 pinch / 1g. (yes)

Cooking instructions:
Heat oil and roast short the small cucumbers. Add Mustard seeds, coriander, cardamom and salt. Add water.
Simmer for 10-15 min. Puree and decorate with fresh chopped sage.

9.38 Fast polenta with avocado and spring onion

Good to fight inflammations, swelling, pain. Forcing spleen and stomach, lets urine and bile juice flow, dissolves stagnation. Includes unsaturated fatty acids, antioxidativ.
Cooking time approx. 10 min
Calories p. portion: 450
2 portions
Allergens:

Quantity of ingredients:
Corn (fast polenta) 1 cup / 120g. (yes)
Water 1 1/2 cups / 240g. (yes)
Olive oil 1 table spoon / 15g. (yes)
Salt 1 pinch / 1g. (yes)
Pepper (ground) 1 pinch / 0,5g. (yes)

Lemon juice 1 dash / 3g. (yes)
Onion (spring onion) 2 pieces / 40g. (yes)
Avocado 1/2 piece / 150g. (yes)
Turmeric (yellow root) 1 pinch / 1g. (yes)
Basil (fresh) 1 teaspoon / 2g. (yes)

Cooking instructions:
Heat water, add oil, lemon and spices.
When the water boils, add the polenta while stirring constantly and cook
for 2 minutes.
When the porridge becomes firm, the polenta is ready.
Add diced avocado and sliced spring onion to the polenta. Sprinkle
fresh basil on it.

9.39 Fennel with roasted walnuts

Forcing spleen, detoxifying, reduces inflammation, improves blood
circulation, improves medication effect, stimulates appetite, antioxidativ,
promotes digestion, stimulates, dissolves stagnation.
Cooking time approx. 20 min
Calories p. portion: 342
4 portions
Allergens: HO

Quantity of ingredients:
Fennel 4 pieces / 800g. (yes)
Nutmeg 1 pinch / 1g. (yes)
Ginger fresh 1/2 teaspoon / 1g. (yes)
Salt 1 pinch / 1g. (yes)
White wine 1/2 cup / 125g. (little)
Peppers powder 1 pinch / 1g. (yes)
Olive oil 2 table spoons / 40g. (yes)
Walnuts 2 table spoons / 35g. (yes)
Water 1 1/2 cups / 220g. (yes)
Corn Grease (Polenta) 1 cup / 120g. (yes)
Salt 1 pinch / 1g. (yes)

Cooking instructions:
Heat very little water in a pot; Fry the fennel in strips. Add Nutmeg, a
little grated ginger, add salt, a dash of white wine, rose paprika.
Simmer until the vegetables are cooked, but still crisp; stir in a little olive
oil; sprinkle with roasted walnuts.
Stir the polenta into a pot of hot water, stirring constantly, until the

polenta has the desired consistency. Salt.
Pull the polenta off the fire and let it swell for about 10 minutes.

9.40 Fine Russian borscht

Strengths spleen and stomach, strengthens the heart, stimulates
digestion, reduces blood pressure, strengthens immune system. For
strengthening after diseases. Good to fight bloating, cramping in
gastrointestinal complaints.
Cooking time approx. 30 min
Calories p. portion: 172
6 portions
Allergens: AGLO

Quantity of ingredients:
Red beet 5/8 oz / 200g. (yes)
Sunflower oil 1 table spoon / 10g. (little)
Onion (shallot) 2 pieces / 40g. (yes)
Carrot 2 pieces / 140g. (yes)
Celery root 1 piece / 500g. (yes)
Parsley root 1 piece / 150g. (yes)
Leek 1/8 lbs - 2oz / 50g. (yes)
Basic recipe for a vegetable soup (nutritious) 3 cups / 650g. (yes)
Bay leaf 1 Leaf / 0,2g. (yes)
Juniper berry 2 pieces / 2g. (yes)
Nutmeg 1 pinch / 1g. (yes)
Savoy cabbage / kale 5/8 oz / 200g. (yes)
Salt 1 pinch / 1g. (yes)
Pepper (ground) 1 pinch / 0,5g. (yes)
Ground 1 pinch / 1g. (yes)
Red wine 1/2 cup / 125g. (little)
Sour cream 15% fat 1 table spoon / 10g. (little)
Dill 1 teaspoon / 10g. (yes)
White bread (wheat bread) 6 slices / 120g. (little)

Cooking instructions:
Fry some beetroot in oil. Fry the onions, carrots, celery, parsley root
and leek well in another pan. Add the stock and the wine; then add bay
leaves, juniper berries and nutmeg and simmer for 15 minutes. Remove
the bay leaf and puree everything.
Heat more broth separately, simmer the steamed beetroot in it. Add
cabbage or white cabbage after half the cooking time and let it steep. At
the end, add the pureed vegetables and season with salt, pepper,

ground cumin and a little red wine. Garnish with some sour cream and finely chopped dill in the plate. Serve with a slice of white bread.

9.41 Fish soup with rosemary

Promotes spleen and liver, reduces blood pressure, strengthens immune system, prevents cancer, reduces radiation damage, has little cholesterol and is protein rich, improves blood circulation, increases appetite. Antioxidant, forcing spleen, dissolves stagnation.
Cooking time approx. 30 min
Calories p. portion: 271
4 portions
Allergens: DLO

Quantity of ingredients:
Basic recipe for a fish soup 2 cup / 500g. (yes)
Rosemary 1/2 bunch / 7g. (yes)
Onion (spring onion) 1 piece / 20g. (yes)
Olive oil 2 table spoons / 35g. (yes)
Fish pieces mixed (fresh water) 5/8 lbs - 8oz / 250g. (recommended)
Carrot 1 piece / 120g. (yes)
Parsnip 1 piece / 180g. (yes)
Celery root 1 slice / 20g. (yes)
Salt 1 pinch / 1g. (yes)
Peppercorns 2 pieces / 1g. (yes)
Garlic 1 clove / 3g. (yes)

Cooking instructions:
Fry the onion and garlic in oil. Add fish broth. Add diced carrots, parsnips and celery. Season with salt and peppercorns. Simmer the soup on a low heat for 25 minutes.
Wash the fish, drizzle with lemon juice, divide into pieces and add to the soup with the pink rosemary. Cook for 5 min on low heat.
Add the chives and parsley and season the soup with the salt.

9.42 Fried asparagus with rocket

Diuretic, improves blood circulation, stimulates digestion, forcing spleen, promotes weight loss. Good to fight immunodeficiency, loss of appetite, arteriosclerosis, bladder weakness, anemia.
Cooking time approx. 15 min
Calories p. portion: 149
3 portions
Allergens: G

Quantity of ingredients:
Butter organic 1 table spoon / 20g. (little)
Asparagus (green or white) 1,1 lbs / 500g. (yes)
Pepper (ground) 1 pinch / 0,5g. (yes)
Salt 1 pinch / 1g. (yes)
Lemon 1/4 piece / 12g. (yes)
Rucola 2 handful / 30g. (yes)
Potato 3/4 lbs / 300g. (yes)

Cooking instructions:
Melt a piece of butter in a hot pan; cut the peeled asparagus into pieces
of 3 to 4 cm, fry for about 10 minutes until tender, but crisp. Sprinkle
with freshly ground pepper, salt, add a few drops of lemon juice or finely
grated lemon zest, finely shredded rucola leaves.
Cook the potatoes in plenty of salted water, then peel.

9.43 Hearty polenta mash

Strengths spleen and stomach, promotes watering, promotes digestion,
detoxifying, promotes perspiration, reduces blood lipids, stimulates,
dissolves stagnation, stimulates appetite, dissolves stagnation.
Cooking time approx. 10 min
Calories p. portion: 262
2 portions
Allergens:

Quantity of ingredients:
Corn Grease (Polenta) 1 cup / 120g. (yes)
Onion (spring onion) 2 pieces / 40g. (yes)
Ginger fresh 1/2 teaspoon / 2g. (yes)
Nutmeg 1 pinch / 1g. (yes)
Salt 1 pinch / 1g. (yes)
Olive oil 1 table spoon / 10g. (yes)
Turmeric (yellow root) 1 pinch / 1g. (yes)
Water 1 1/2 cups / 240g. (yes)

Cooking instructions:
Stir in the polenta in boiling water and let it swell for 7 min. Add green
onion, grated ginger, turmeric, nutmeg, salt and olive oil and wait for 3
more minutes.

9.44 Hummus (Chickpeas mash)

Relaxes breast pressure, moisturizer dry skin, helps to fight incontinence, antioxidativ. Stimulates liver function, detoxifying, stimulates the immune system, dissolves stagnation.
Cooking time approx. 2 hours
Calories p. portion: 542
2 portions
Allergens: N

Quantity of ingredients:
Chickpeas 1 1/2 cups / 240g. (yes)
Wakame 1 teaspoon (grated) / 2g. (yes)
Ginger fresh 1/4 teaspoon / 1g. (yes)
Rosemary 1 pinch / 0,5g. (yes)
Sesame paste (Tahini) 1 table spoon / 10g. (yes)
Olive oil 2 table spoons / 20g. (yes)
Lemon juice 1 dach / 2g. (yes)
Water upon need / g. (yes)
Garlic 1 clove (scraped) / 2g. (yes)
Parsley 1 teaspoon (chopped) / 2g. (yes)
Peppers 1 pinch / 0,2g. (yes)
Curcuma 1 pinch / 0,2g. (yes)
Coriander 1 pinch / 0,2g. (yes)
Cardamom 1 pinch / 0,2g. (yes)
Pepper (ground) 1 pinch / 0,2g. (yes)
Salt (herbal) 1/2 teaspoon / 2g. (yes)

Cooking instructions:
Soak chickpeas overnight or for at least 6 hours, pour off soaking water, boil in fresh water for about 1 to 1 ½ hours with a little seaweed and ginger, allow to cool.
Seasoning with a few splashes of lemon juice and parsley.
Add the pepper, garlic cut into small pieces or pressed, more or less coriander and cardamom powder, little chilly powder as desired, tahin and olive oil.

Puree all ingredients together. Depending on the consistency, add water. It should be a smooth paste.
Spread on cereal, crackers or toasted bread or enjoy with salad.

9.45 Hungarian rice salad

Promotes digestion, helps to digest fat, supports urination, reduces blood pressure, strengthens kidney and bladder, diuretic, warming the body from the inside, expands blood vessels, strengthens the muscles, regulates internal organs functions.
Cooking time approx. 25 min
Calories p. portion: 421
2 portions
Allergens: GM

Quantity of ingredients:
Rice (whole grain) 1/2 cup / 60g. (yes)
Water 3 cups / 300g. (yes)
Salt 1 pinch / 0,3g. (yes)
Tomato 1/4 lbs - 4oz / 100g. (yes)
Peppers 1/8 lbs - 2oz / 50g. (yes)
Champignon 1 oz / 30g. (yes)
Edam cheese 1 oz / 30g. (yes)
Yogurt (natural, 1.5% fat) 1/8 lbs - 2oz / 45g. (yes)
Salt 1 pinch / 1g. (yes)
Herbs various 1 table spoon / 8g. (yes)
Rapeseed oil 2 table spoons / 20g. (yes)
Mustard 1 teaspoon / 3g. (yes)
Pepper (ground) 1 pinch / 0,2g. (yes)

Cooking instructions:
Pour the rice into plenty of boiling salt water and let it drain gently. Wash tomatoes and peppers and core. Cut both in to small cubes. Peel the mushrooms (from the tin or with rapeseed oil for a short time) and cut the cheese into small cubes and add to the rice. Prepare the marinade and mix with the ingredients, refrigerate and leave for at least an hour.

9.46 Italian champignon rice

Refreshing and nourishing. Promotes digestion and is good to fight high blood pressure. Strengthens spleen and stomach, strengthens the muscles, improves blood circulation, encourages growth, dissolves stagnation.
Cooking time approx. 25 min
Calories p. portion: 256
4 portions
Allergens: G

Quantity of ingredients:
Rice round grain 1 1/2 cups / 240g. (yes)
Water 2 cup / 450g. (yes)
Pepper (ground) 1 pinch / 0,2g. (yes)
Salt 1 pinch / 0,5g. (yes)
Lemon juice 1 dash / 2g. (yes)
Pepper powder (hot) 1 pinch / 0,2g. (yes)
Champignon 5/8 lbs - 8oz / 250g. (yes)
Olive oil 1 teaspoon / 3g. (yes)
Chives 1 teaspoon / 5g. (yes)
Parmesan 2 table spoons / 20g. (little)

Cooking instructions:
Put the round grain rice in cold water 1:6 and cook.
Add ground pepper, salt, plenty of lemon juice, rose paprika, a little olive oil or butter and mix well.
Carefully add in mushrooms, chives or the green parts of the spring onion, and carefully add in some grated Parmesan cheese.
Goes well with vegetables and tofu dishes, tomato sauce dishes.

9.47 Japanese algae soup

Reduces blood pressure, strengthens immune system, prevents cancer, reduces radiation damage. Promotes digestion. Detoxifying and stimulates the immune system.
Cooking time approx. 20 min
Calories p. portion: 47
3 portions
Allergens:

Quantity of ingredients:
Wakame 1 oz / 25g. (yes)
Water 2 cup / 450g. (yes)
Onion (shallot) 1-2 pcs. / 30g. (yes)
Radish (white, green, purple-red) 1/8 lbs - 2oz / 50g. (yes)
Carrot 2 pieces / 180g. (yes)
Miso 2 table spoons / 20g. (yes)
Parsley 2 table spoons / 20g. (yes)
Onion (spring onion) 1 table spoon (sliced)

Cooking instructions:
Soak wakame in water for a few minutes, remove and bring the water to the boil. Add finely chopped onions and wakame, radishes and carrots, cut into thin strips, and simmer for another 10 minutes. Dissolve miso in a little cooled cooking water and add it at the end. Sprinkle with parsley and spring onions.

9.48 Kohlrabi in chervil sauce with potatoes

Reduces inflammation, lowers cholesterol, conducts bowel winds, strengthens immune system, promotes weight loss. Good to fight loss of appetite, flatulence, high blood pressure, diabetes, diarrhea.
Cooking time approx. 1 hour
Calories p. portion: 188
4 portions
Allergens: GL

Quantity of ingredients:
Potato 6 pieces / 450g. (yes)
Basic recipe for a vegetable soup (nutritious) 1 cup / 300g. (yes)
Potato 1/4 lbs - 4oz / 100g. (yes)
Nutmeg 1 pinch / 0,2g. (yes)
Lemon peel 1/2 teaspoon / 2g. (yes)
Ginger fresh 1/2 teaspoon / 2g. (yes)
Lovage 1/2 teaspoon / 2g. (yes)
Kohlrabi 3/4 lbs / 300g. (recommended)
Salt 1 pinch / 1g. (yes)
Pepper (ground) 1 pinch / 0,2g. (yes)
Sour cream 15% fat 2 table spoons / 30g. (little)
Chervil dried 1 Bunch / 80g. (yes)

Cooking instructions:
Boil the potatoes in salted water.
Bring half of the vegetable stock to boil. Add the diced potatoes, nutmeg, lemon zest, ginger and lovage. Cover the potatoes and cook for about 10 minutes until soft and puree them with a blender until they are smooth.
Bring remaining vegetable stock to boil. Cut kohlrabi into cubes and add, cover and cook for about 8 minutes. Stir in the potato sauce and heat everything briefly.
Puree with the mixing stick chervil and sour cream. Mix the chervil cream with the kohlrabi vegetables.
Serve with the cooked, peeled potatoes.

9.49 Leek soup with almond mash

Warming and nourishing. Promotes sweating, dissolves stagnation.
Little laxative. Astringent, antibacterial, invigorating, calming, blood-
forming, blood detoxifying, lowering blood sugar. Promotes digestion,
strengthens lung, promotes spleen and kidney.
Cooking time approx. 20 min
Calories p. portion: 115
4 portions
Allergens: HN

Quantity of ingredients:
Water 2 cup / 480g. (yes)
Sugar cane sugar 1 pinch / 0,3g. (little)
Leek 2 pieces / 400g. (yes)
Salt 1 pinch / 0,5g. (yes)
Lemon juice 1/2 piece / 15g. (yes)
Rosemary 1 Twig / 3g. (yes)
Pepper powder (hot) Alternative to rosemary / g. (yes)
Potato flour 1 table spoon / 8g. (yes)
Almond puree 2 table spoons / 20g. (yes)
Sesame oil few drops / 1g. (yes)
Pepper white (ground) 1 pinch / 0,2g. (yes)

Cooking instructions:
Add a pinch of sugar to hot water, add chopped leeks and a pinch of
salt; simmer until the leek is half cooked; season with lemon juice, fresh
rosemary or rose paprika.

Dissolve potato flour separately in cold water; thicken the soup with it.

Add almond purée, a few drops of toasted sesame oil, pepper and
simmer until the leek is cooked.

Variant (TCM):
Add mushrooms; they build up juices and soften the yangling effect of
the leeks.

9.50 Lentils and rice stew

Promotes spleen and kidney, is very nutritious, reduces blood pressure, strengthens immune system. Good to fight blood circulation disorders, thromboses, risk of embolism, high blood pressure, a headache. Strengthens heart and kidney, diuretic, calms the stomach, promotes digestion.
Cooking time approx. 25 min
Calories p. portion: 232
3 portions
Allergens: LNO

Quantity of ingredients:
Lentils 1/4 lbs - 4oz / 100g. (recommended)
Water 5 cups / 500g. (yes)
Rice variety any 1 cup / 120g. (yes)
Sesame oil 1 table spoon / 10g. (yes)
Carrot 2 pieces / 150g. (yes)
Celery sticks 2 rods / 20g. (yes)
Cumin (Caraway seed) 1 pinch / 0,2g. (yes)
Salt 1 pinch / 0,5g. (yes)
Vinegar (Apple vinegar) 1 dash / 2g. (yes)
Parsley 2 table spoons / 18g. (yes)

Cooking instructions:
Soak the dry lentils the day before.
Heat sesame oil in a hot pot; cut carrot and celery into small pieces and sauté; add rice, a pinch of cumin and lentils and heat till it boils.
If the lenses are soft, add salt; season with a little vinegar and garnish with parsley.

Variant: In summer you can omit the cumin and add fresh green peas, Chinese cabbage or celery.

9.51 Marinated cod on pumpkin puree

Reduces inflammation, improves digestion, promotes spleen, lung, stomach and kidneys, diuretic, reduces blood glucose, good to fight constipation and flatulence, dissolves stagnation.
Cooking time approx. 2 hours
Calories p. portion: 202
4 portions
Allergens: DG

Quantity of ingredients:
Potato 6 pieces / 400g. (yes)
Pumpkin 5/8 oz / 200g. (yes)
Onion white 1 piece / 50g. (yes)
Oregano dried 1/2 teaspoon / 1g. (yes)
Lemon juice 1/2 piece / 15g. (yes)
Salt 1 pinch / 1g. (yes)
Pepper (ground) 1 pinch / 0,3g. (yes)
Créme fraiche cheese 2 table spoons / 30g. (little)
Yogurt (natural, 1.5% fat) 3/8 lbs - 6oz / 150g. (yes)
Oregano dried 1/4 teaspoon / 1g. (yes)
Basil (fresh) 1/2 teaspoon / 2g. (yes)
Cod 3/4 lbs / 300g. (recommended)
Salt 1 pinch / 1g. (yes)
Pepper (ground) 1 pinch / 0,3g. (yes)
Olive oil 1 teaspoon / 3g. (yes)

Cooking instructions:
Mix yoghurt with oregano, basil and thyme.
Wash the fish fillets, pat dry, place in a flat shape and pour over the marinade. Leave 2 hours in refrigerator.

Cook the potatoes in salted water until soft and peel.

Sauté the onion in oil until glassy, add the diced pumpkin and cook for about 10 min. Add oregano, lemon juice, salt, pepper and crème fraiche and puree with the blender.

Remove fish fillets from the marinade, drain, pat dry and salt. Coat a coated grill pan with 2 teaspoons of oil. Roast the fish fillets on both sides for 3 - 4 minutes and arrange with the potatoes on the pumpkin puree.

9.52 Marinated turkey with cashew nuts from the wok

Strengthens blood, strengthens bone marrow, for the drainage of the body overweight and high blood pressure. Promotes digestion, helps to digest fat, supports urination, reduces blood pressure.
Cooking time approx. 30 min
Calories p. portion: 319
4 portions
Allergens: ELNO

Quantity of ingredients:
Turkey breast meat 3/4 lbs / 300g. (yes)
Sake until covered / g. (yes)
Sesame oil 2 table spoons / 30g. (yes)
Ginger fresh 1/2 teaspoon / 2g. (yes)
Salt 1 pinch / 0,5g. (yes)
Lemon 1/2 piece / 15g. (yes)
Red wine 1/2 cup / 125g. (little)
Sugar cane sugar 1 pinch / 1g. (little)
Onion (spring onion) 4 pieces / 80g. (yes)
Tomato 2 pieces / 100g. (yes)
Basic recipe for a chicken soup (warming) 1 cup / 120g. (yes)
Cashews 2 table spoons / 16g. (yes)
Soy sauce 1 dash / 2g. (yes)
Rice Basmati 1 cup / 120g. (yes)
Water 6 cups / 400g. (yes)
Salt 1 pinch / 0,5g. (yes)

Cooking instructions:
Preparation: cover sliced turkey meat with rice wine; marinate overnight or for a few hours.

Then: strain and drain well; heat sesame oil in a hot wok; fry finely chopped ginger; sauté the meat for a short time; add the marinade; add salt, lemon juice, red wine or rose paprika; let the meat soak in the sauce for 2 - 3 minutes; then exhaust it; add some sugar to the sauce in the wok; add a few spring onions (the white parts), a pinch of salt, chopped tomatoes, 1 cup of chicken broth; simmer so that the onions are still crisp.
Roasted cashews, add the cashews and the meat to the sauce and heat; season with soy sauce; stir in the green of the chopped green onions.
Boil the rice with the water, salt and cook for about 20 minutes.

9.53 Melanzani with olive oil and turmeric

improves blood circulation, reduces inflammation, relieves pain, promotes digestion, helps to digest fat, supports urination, reduces blood pressure.
Cooking time approx. 30 min
Calories p. portion: 432
2 portions
Allergens: A

Quantity of ingredients:
Aubergine 2 pieces / 300g. (yes)
Olive oil 4 table spoons / 60g. (yes)
Tomato 4 pieces / 200g. (yes)
Turmeric (yellow root) 1/2 teaspoon / 1g. (yes)
Ground 1 pinch / 1g. (yes)
Salt 1 pinch / 1g. (yes)
White bread (wheat bread) 4 slices / 80g. (little)

Cooking instructions:
Cut the melanzani into slices and spread them with the tomatoes on a
baking tray. Sprinkle with olive oil and then with turmeric, caraway and
salt. Bake them in the tube 20 min.
Serve with the white bread.

9.54 Millet with pears

Refreshing and nourishing, promotes digestion, supports urination,
good to fight cough, promotes perspiration, reduces blood lipids,
stimulates, dissolves stagnation, forces liver, strengthens the muscles,
lowers cholesterol, antiparasitic.
Cooking time approx. 35 min
Calories p. portion: 213
5 portions
Allergens: G

Quantity of ingredients:
Millet 1 cup / 120g. (yes)
Water 1 1/2 cups / 200g. (yes)
Grape juice red 1 1/2 cups / 240g. (yes)
Pear 4 pieces / 600g. (yes)
Ginger fresh 1/2 teaspoon / 2g. (yes)
Salt 1 pinch / 1g. (yes)
Acerola fruit nectar or powder 1 teaspoon / 2g. (recommended)
Cocoa 1 pinch / 1g. (yes)
Sunflower seeds 2 table spoons / 4g. (yes)
Barley malt 1/2 teaspoon / 2g. (yes)
Cream, sweet 30% 2 teaspoons / 20g. (little)

Cooking instructions:
Simmer the millet for 5 min and let it swell for another 30 min.

Then: In a hot pot, heat some grape juice; add chopped pears, very little grated ginger, a pinch of salt, acerola, a pinch of cocoa and sauté briefly; add the boiled millet, sunflower seeds, some barley malt to taste, 1 tsp cream per serving or a little butter.

9.55 Minestrone

Diuretic, Supports urination. Promotes digestion, Helps to digest fat, Supports urination, reduces blood pressure, strengthens immune system.
Cooking time approx. 30 min
Calories p. portion: 211
4 portions
Allergens: GL

Quantity of ingredients:
Onion (shallot) 2 pieces / 40g. (yes)
Sunflower oil 1 teaspoon / 10g. (little)
Water 2 cup / 480g. (yes)
Carrot 2 pieces / 120g. (yes)
Savoy cabbage / kale Handful / 15g. (yes)
Beans (green, fresh) Handful / 20g. (recommended)
Celery sticks 3 pieces / 20g. (yes)
Peas, green 4 table spoons / 30g. (yes)
Zucchini 1 piece / 200g. (yes)
Rice variety any 1 cup / 120g. (yes)
Bay leaf 3 leaves / 1g. (yes)
Sunflower oil 1 table spoon / 10g. (little)
Salt 1 pinch / 1g. (yes)
Tomato 3 pieces / 150g. (yes)
Thyme 1 Twig / 3g. (yes)
Parmesan 2 table spoons / 18g. (little)
Basil 4 leaves / 2g. (yes)

Cooking instructions:
Fry the onion in oil in a glassy saucepan and add water. Add vegetables, rice and salt and simmer gently. If the vegetables are firm, add tomatoes, a small sprig of thyme, basil and bay leaf and leave to simmer. Serve with Parmesan.

9.56 Mung bean stew

Relieves excessive thirst, supports urination, reduces blood lipids, relieves allergies. Strengthens spleen and stomach, strengthens the muscles. Lowers cholesterol, antiparasitic. Stimulates liver function, detoxifying.
Cooking time approx. 2 hours
Calories p. portion: 665
2 portions
Allergens:

Quantity of ingredients:
Mung bean 5/8 lbs - 8oz - 500g / 300g. (yes)
Sunflower oil 2 table spoons / 30g. (little)
Amaranth 1/2 teaspoon / 2g. (recommended)
Fennel seeds ground 1/2 teaspoon / 2g. (yes)
Cumin (Caraway seed) 1/2 teaspoon / 2g. (yes)
Coriander 1/2 teaspoon / 2g. (yes)
Rice round grain 1/2 cup / 60g. (yes)
Water 3 cups / 300g. (yes)
Ginger fresh 1 inch / 3g. (yes)
Kombu seaweed (Saccharina japonica) 1 inch / 2g. (yes)
Salt 1 pinch / 0,5g. (yes)
Parsley 1 table spoon / 3g. (yes)

Cooking instructions:
Soak mung beans overnight.
Heat sunflower oil in a hot pot. Stir in the amaranth, fennel seeds, cumin and coriander and fry briefly.
admit basmati rice, some ginger and mung beans and roast briefly.
Pour water and heat till it boils.
Add a piece of kombu alga and salt.
Simmer for 1-1/2 hours.
Garnish with parsley or coriander.

9.57 Oven potatoes with celery-curd cheese (quark)

Promotes spleen, reduces Inflammation, improves digestion, regenerates skin, supports urination, lowers cholesterol.
Cooking time approx. 30 min
Calories p. portion: 304
2 portions
Allergens: GL

Quantity of ingredients:
Celery root 3 oz / 80g. (yes)
Basic recipe for a vegetable soup (nutritious) 1/2 cup / 100g. (yes)
Ground caraway 1 pinch / 0,2g. (yes)
Lemon peel 1/2 teaspoon / 1g. (yes)
Salt 1 pinch / 1g. (yes)
Pepper (ground) 1 pinch / 0,2g. (yes)
Lemon juice 1 teaspoon / 3g. (yes)
Curd cheese 20% 5/8 oz / 200g. (yes)
Créme fraiche cheese 1/2 teaspoon / 5g. (little)
Potato 6 pieces / 400g. (yes)
Olive oil 2 teaspoons / 5g. (yes)
Salt 1 pinch / 1g. (yes)

Cooking instructions:
Celery-curd cheese:
Mix celery with vegetable broth according to basic recipe, caraway and lemon peel. Cook for about 8 minutes until the celery is soft and the vegetable broth almost evaporated. Mix the celery vegetable broth with the lemon juice, finely, and stir until smooth. Season with salt and pepper.

Baked potatoes:
Preheat oven to 200 °C / 400 °F.
Brush the potatoes well, halve them, and place them on a baking tray with the cut surface facing up. Lightly salt the surfaces and sprinkle with oil. Fry the potatoes in the oven for about 25 minutes.
Serve the celery plug to the potatoes.

9.58 Oyster mushrooms with asparagus

Forces, reduces inflammation, improves digestion, lowers cholesterol, strengthens kidney, stimulates liver function, improves blood circulation, improves medication effect, increases appetite.
Cooking time approx. 30 min
Calories p. portion: 316
4 portions
Allergens: GH

Quantity of ingredients:
Onion white 1 piece / 50g. (yes)
Butter organic 2 table spoons / 40g. (little)
Oyster mushroom 3/4 lbs / 300g. (yes)
Sake 2 table spoons / 40g. (yes)
Parsley 2 table spoons / 40g. (yes)
Walnuts 2 table spoons / 60g. (yes)
Asparagus (green or white) 1,1 lbs / 500g. (yes)
Salt 1 pinch / 1g. (yes)
Sugar white 1 pinch / 0,1g. (little)
Potato 1 lbs / 500g. (yes)
Salt (herbal) 1 pinch / 1g. (yes)

Cooking instructions:
Cook organically grown potatoes with the skin, otherwise prepare peeled boiled potatoes. Boil the asparagus in salted water with a pinch of sugar and salt. (You can cook an old roll that absorbs the bittering substances.)
Slightly sauté the chopped onions in a pan in the butter before frying the oyster mushrooms cut into the same pan.
Stew 15 minutes, stirring several times. Add the sake, walnuts and parsley and simmer on low heat while you drain the potatoes and asparagus. Finally, sprinkle some herbal salt over it.
If no fresh asparagus is available, asparagus can be used in jars.

9.59 Parsley cream sauce

Reduces blood pressure, forcing spleen, dissolves stagnation, improves digestion, lowers cholesterol. Stimulates liver function, detoxifying.
Cooking time approx. 25 min
Calories p. portion: 118
2 portions
Allergens: GL

Quantity of ingredients:
Basic recipe for a vegetable soup (nutritious) 3/4 lbs / 300g. (yes)
Potato 1/4 lbs - 4oz / 100g. (yes)
Parsley 1 Bunch / 15g. (yes)
Nutmeg 1 pinch / 0,5g. (yes)
Coriander 1/2 teaspoon / 1g. (yes)
Sour cream 15% fat 1/8 lbs - 2oz / 50g. (little)
Fennel seeds ground 1/2 teaspoon / 1g. (yes)
Ginger powder 1 pinch / 0,5g. (yes)

Cooking instructions:
Broth the vegetables soup according to the basic recipe with peeled, diced potatoes, half of the finely chopped parsley and nutmeg. Cover and simmer until the potatoes are tender.

Using the blender, puree the vegetable broth, potatoes, remaining freshly chopped parsley, fennel, ginger and sour cream into a smooth sauce.

9.60 Pear compote

Promotes digestion, supports urination.
Cooking time approx. 20 min
Calories p. portion: 100
3 portions
Allergens:

Quantity of ingredients:
Water 1 1/2 cups / 240g. (yes)
Pear 4 / 500g. (yes)

Cooking instructions:
Halve organic pears. Cores and skin can be used. Pear in the pot and add water. Simmer for up to 20 minutes until pears are tender.

9.61 Plum Cake

Cancer preventive effect, dehydrates the body, stimulates digestion and binds fats in the intestine, good to fight loss of appetite, flatulence, inflammatory bowel disease, obesity, gout, stomach ulcers, stomach cramps, rheumatism, heartburn. Relieves pain, detoxifying, bactericide.
Cooking time approx. 1 hour
Calories p. portion: 502
6 portions
Allergens: AG

Quantity of ingredients:
Curd cheese 20% 5/8 oz / 200g. (yes)
Wheat flour 7/8 lbs / 400g. (yes)
Cow's milk (whole milk 3.5% fat) 6 table spoons / 70g. (little)
Rapeseed oil 6 table spoons / 70g. (yes)
Honey 8 table spoons / 100g. (yes)
Baking powder 1 package / 3g. (yes)

Salt 1 pinch / 1g. (yes)
Cinnamon ground 1 teaspoon / 3g. (yes)
Plums 2,2 lbs / 1000g. (yes)

Cooking instructions:
Mix the flour, curd cheese, milk, oil, honey, salt and baking powder into a smooth dough. Keep the dough cool for 15 minutes to cool.
Lay out baking paper on a baking sheet and press the dough out to a bottom.
Now spread the plums evenly.
Sprinkle the cake with the cinnamon and bake for about 40 minutes at 190 ° C/374 °F.

9.62 Polenta with peach

Relieves fatigue, forcing spleen, diuretic, strengthens the defense, good to fight fungi infections, lets urine and bile juice flow, prevents the aging process, strengthens brain cells.
Cooking time approx. 20 min
Calories p. portion: 197
3 portions
Allergens:

Quantity of ingredients:
Water 1 1/2 cups / 240g. (yes)
Corn Grease (Polenta) 1 cup / 120g. (yes)
Peaches 2-3 pieces / 400g. (yes)
Vanilla pod 1 pinch / 1g. (yes)
Cinnamon ground 1 pinch / 1g. (yes)

Cooking instructions:
Pour the polenta into a pan of hot water with constant stirring until the polenta has the desired consistency. Pull the polenta from the fire and let it soak for 10 minutes.

Wash fresh peaches and cut into quarters. Pour into the finished polenta the peaches, add the vanilla and add Chili to taste, stir and let it go for 3 minutes.

Winter varieties: Pickled fruit, pear, apples

9.63 Polenta with ratatouille

Forcing spleen and stomach, lets urine and bile juice flow. Diuretic, supports urination. Promotes digestion, helps to digest fat, supports urination, reduces blood pressure.
Cooking time approx. 30 min
Calories p. portion: 226
4 portions
Allergens: G

Quantity of ingredients:
Corn Grease (Polenta) 1 cup / 120g. (yes)
Water 1 1/2 cups / 240g. (yes)
Aubergine 1 piece (large) / 200g. (yes)
Zucchini 2 pieces / 500g. (yes)
Onion white 2 pieces / 120g. (yes)
Tomato 2 pieces (blended) / 200g. (yes)
Olive oil 2 table spoons / 20g. (yes)
Salt 1 pinch / 0,5g. (yes)
Parsley 1 table spoon (chopped) / 8g. (yes)
Thyme 1/2 teaspoon / 1g. (yes)
Onion (spring onion) 2 table spoons (chopped) / 12g. (yes)
Basil 4 leaves / 2g. (yes)
Parmesan 2 table spoons / 20g. (little)

Cooking instructions:
Use double the amount of water to polenta, add salt and oil and heat till it boils. Stir in polenta, stirring constantly.
Take off the fire and let it swell for 20 minutes. Meanwhile, cut the onion, fry in a saucepan with hot oil. Add the diced zucchini, tomatoes and melanzani and simmer for about 20 minutes. Add basil, thyme, salt.
Coat baking tray with oil, apply polenta evenly and wait until it gets stronger.
Add the cooked ratatouille to polenta, portion and then put in the oven for a few minutes (possibly with grated parmesan).
Sprinkle with fresh parsley and finely chopped spring onion.
The valuable tip: The Polenta sections are ideal for on the go.

9.64 Potato with dandelion salad

Promotes spleen, reduces inflammation, improves digestion, regenerates skin, supports urinating, lowers cholesterol, detoxifying, reduces inflammation, forcing spleen and digestive system, detoxifying, dissolves stagnation.
Cooking time approx. 25 min
Calories p. portion: 162
2 portions
Allergens:

Quantity of ingredients:
Potato 5/8 lbs - 8oz / 250g. (yes)
Onion white 1/2 piece / 20g. (yes)
Sunflower oil 1 table spoon / 10g. (little)
Dandelion (young plants) 1/4 lbs - 4oz / 125g. (yes)
Salt 1 pinch / 1g. (yes)
Pepper white (ground) 1 pinch / 0,5g. (yes)

Cooking instructions:
Cook the potatoes in salted water and cut into thin slices. Finely chop the onion. Now season the potatoes with oil, salt and pepper and add the dandelion and mix.

9.65 Potato-basil soup

Reduces inflammation, improves digestion, supports urination, lowers cholesterol, reduces blood pressure, strengthens immune system, prevents cancer, reduces radiation damage, antioxidativ, dissolves stagnation.
Cooking time approx. 25 min
Calories p. portion: 96
4 portions
Allergens: L

Quantity of ingredients:
Water 2 cups / 450g. (yes)
Potato 4 pieces / 200g. (yes)
Carrot 2 pieces / 100g. (yes)
Celery root 1 piece / 500g. (yes)
Pepper (ground) 1 pinch / 0,5g. (yes)
Ground 1 pinch / 1g. (yes)
Garlic 1 clove / 3g. (yes)
Salt 1 pinch / 1g. (yes)

Lemon 1 teaspoon / 3g. (yes)
Basil (fresh) 1 Bunch / 50g. (yes)
Peppers powder 1 pinch / 1g. (yes)
Sugar cane sugar 1 pinch / 1g. (little)
Olive oil 1 table spoon / 10g. (yes)

Cooking instructions:
Peeled and chopped 4 medium potatoes in a pot of hot water and 2 chopped medium carrots, a piece of celery root, a pinch of pepper, a pinch of ground cumin, crushed a small clove of garlic, a pinch of salt, 1 teaspoon of lemon juice, simmer until the Vegetables is soft.
Add 1 bunch finely chopped basil into one half of the soup and puree everything; stir in the other half of the basil; with rose paprika, a pinch of whole cane sugar, 1 tablespoon of olive oil or butter, freshly ground pepper, salt to taste.

9.66 Potatoes with curd cheese sauce

Improves digestion, supports urination, lowers cholesterol. Good to fight weakness, belching, diabetes, acute or chronic obstruction of the bowel, skin problems, bloating, cramping in gastrointestinal complaints.
Cooking time approx. 45 min
Calories p. portion: 414
6 portions
Allergens: G

Quantity of ingredients:
Potato 2,2 lbs / 1000g. (yes)
Curd cheese 20% 1,1 lbs / 500g. (yes)
Cream, sweet 30% 5/8 oz / 200g. (little)
Edam cheese 3 oz / 80g. (yes)
Dill 1 Bunch / 100g. (yes)
Corn germ oil 1 teaspoon / 3g. (yes)
Pepper (ground) 1 pinch / 0,2g. (yes)
Salt 1/2 teaspoon / 1g. (yes)
Sunflower seeds 1/8 lbs - 2oz / 40g. (yes)

Cooking instructions:
Wash the potatoes and cook in plenty of water for about 20 minutes. Stir the creamy cheese with the cream and cottage cheese. Wash the sprouts, finely chop. Stir in with the chopped dill. (For the baby, mix 150 g. of pot with the oil.) Mix the rest with pepper, salt and the sunflower seeds. Peel the potatoes, arrange.

9.67 Potatoes with wild garlic-curd cheese

Improves digestion, regenerates skin, supports urination, lowers cholesterol. Helps to fight stomach pressure, belching, diabetes, acute or chronic constipation of the intestine. Improves the flow characteristics of the blood.
Cooking time approx. 20 min
Calories p. portion: 254
2 portions
Allergens: G

Quantity of ingredients:
Potato 3/4 lbs / 300g. (yes)
Salt 1 pinch / 0,1g. (yes)
Wild garlic (garlic spinach) 2 handful / 30g. (yes)
Curd cheese 20% 5/8 lbs - 8oz / 250g. (yes)
Yogurt (natural, 1.5% fat) 2 table spoons / 20g. (yes)
Salt 1 pinch / 1g. (yes)

Cooking instructions:
Cook potatoes in salted water and peel.
Wash he wild garlic leaves and carefully dried and cut into fine strips.
Mix the cottage cheese, yogurt and salt and mix in the chopped wild garlic pieces. Serve with the potatoes.
In the season in which no wild garlic grows the wild garlic pesto can be used.

9.68 Pumpkin slices with spicy rice

Strengthens lungs and spleen, diuretic, reduces blood glucose, protects liver, for the drainage of the body overweight and high blood pressure, harmonizes liver.
Cooking time approx. 45 min
Calories p. portion: 438
4 portions
Allergens: AG

Quantity of ingredients:
Clarified butter 1/2 teaspoon / 5g. (little)
Saffron 1 Sachet / 0,1g. (yes)
Turmeric (yellow root) 1 teaspoon / 2g. (yes)
Rice Basmati 1 cup / 120g. (yes)
Water 1 cup / 120g. (yes)
Salt 1/2 teaspoon / 2g. (yes)

Pumpkin 6-8 slices / 400g. (yes)
Barley flour 1 cup / 10g. (yes)
Breadcrumbs (wheat bread, bread roll) 1 cup / 10g. (yes)
Salt 1/2 teaspoon / 2g. (yes)
Pepper (ground) 1 pinch / 1g. (yes)
Butter organic 1 table spoon / 10g. (little)
Cream, sweet 30% 1 1/2 cup / 300g. (little)
Barley flour 2 table spoons / 20g. (yes)
Chives 2 table spoons / 20g. (yes)
Dill 2 table spoons / 20g. (yes)

Cooking instructions:
Melt the fat in a small saucepan, add saffron and turmeric, lightly roast over medium heat for about 1-2 minutes to allow the aromas to develop (note: the spices should never be burnt). Add the rice for about 2 minutes stir fry, add the salt, stir briefly and add the water, stir and close the pot with a lid. Cook at low to medium heat until the water is almost completely absorbed, then remove from the heat and set aside with the lid still closed and let it swell. Do not stir! When the water is completely absorbed, the rice is ready!

Mix flour, bread crumbs, salt and pepper. Moisten the pumpkin slices with water or mashed egg, turn the slices in the flour mixture and fry gently in butter until golden brown and the pumpkin is soft. Melt the butter in a small saucepan, brown the barley flour in it and remove from heat, add the sour cream, season with salt, pepper, add the chopped herbs and pour the sauce over the fried pumpkin slices. Serve with the rice.

9.69 Pumpkin soup

Promotes digestion, forcing spleen and stomach, reduces blood pressure, strengthens immune system, prevents cancer, reduces radiation damage, improves digestion, regenerates skin, lowers cholesterol, reduces blood glucose, protects liver.
Cooking time approx. 1 hour
Calories p. portion: 105
3 portions
Allergens:

Quantity of ingredients:
Pumpkin 3/4 lbs / 300g. (yes)
Carrot 2 pieces / 100g. (yes)
Potato 2 pieces / 120g. (yes)
Olive oil 1 table spoon / 10g. (yes)
Onion white 1 piece / 50g. (yes)
Water 1 cup / 120g. (yes)
Parsley 1 table spoon / 7g. (yes)
Anise (Common Fennel) 1 pinch / 1g. (yes)
Salt 1 pinch / 1g. (yes)

Cooking instructions:
Add the olive oil to the pan, add the diced pumpkin, diced carrots and potatoes. Roast them shortly, add the finely chopped onion, fill with water, add enough water to cover the vegetables at least 3 finger-widths. Boil at low heat.

Season with sea salt, add small cutted parsley, a pinch of anise (little). Allow to simmer for about 35 minutes. Then purée the soup and add some water, depending on the consistency of the soup.

9.70 Quick zucchini soup

Diuretic, supports urination. Strengthens gastrointestinal function, expands blood vessels, prevents cancer, prevents diseases (in the elderly). Stimulates liver function, detoxifying.
Cooking time approx. 10 min
Calories p. portion: 42
4 portions
Allergens:

Quantity of ingredients:
Zucchini 2-3 pieces / 500g. (yes)
Onion white 1 piece / 50g. (yes)
Corn germ oil 2 table spoons / 6g. (yes)
Parsley 1 table spoon / 7g. (yes)
Chives 1 teaspoon / 3g. (yes)
Water 2 cup / 400g. (yes)

Cooking instructions:
Fry chopped onion in oil. Add sliced zucchini and sauté well. Pour with water. Chop parsley and chives, add and puree everything.

9.71 Refreshing cucumber soup with potatoes

Diuretic, detoxifying, suppresses conversion of sugar into fat, lowers cholesterol, prevents cancer, reduces inflammation, improves digestion, lowers cholesterol, dissolves stagnation, improves blood circulation, stimulates appetite.
Cooking time approx. 15 min
Calories p. portion: 148
3 portions
Allergens: GN

Quantity of ingredients:
Sesame oil 1 table spoon / 10g. (yes)
Potato 4 pieces / 300g. (yes)
Onion (spring onion) 3 pieces / 60g. (yes)
Pepper (ground) 1 pinch / 0,5g. (yes)
Nutmeg 1 pinch / 1g. (yes)
Salt 1 pinch / 1g. (yes)
Lemon 1/2 piece / 25g. (yes)
Cucumber 2 pieces / 500g. (yes)
Cream, sweet 30% 1 table spoon / 10g. (little)
Dill 1 table spoon / 15g. (yes)

Cooking instructions:
Sauté sesame oil, chopped potatoes, plenty of spring onions in a hot pot; add pepper, a little nutmeg, salt, lemon juice, hot water, diced cucumber; simmer for about 10 minutes and then puree; add some sweet cream as you like, fresh dill.

Variation: Add a little chili, oregano, thyme or rosemary to soften the cooling effect.

9.72 Rhubarb and apple jelly

Antioxidants, lots of vitamin C, laxative, relieves pain, detoxifying, warms stomach and spleen, improves blood circulation.
Cooking time approx. 15 min
Calories p. portion: 180
2 portions
Allergens:

Quantity of ingredients:
Rhubarb 5/8 oz / 200g. (yes)
Apple juice (natural cloudy) 1 cup / 300g. (yes)
Corn starch 1 oz / 30g. (yes)
Honey 1/2 oz / 20g. (yes)
Vanilla sugar natural 1 pinch / 0,5g. (yes)
Cinnamon ground 1 pinch / 0,5g. (yes)
Peppermint 2 leaves / 2g. (yes)

Cooking instructions:
Add the cornstarch to a 1/2 cup apple juice.
Simmer the rhubarb in 1 cup of water for 10 min.
Add the remaining apple juice and the cornstarch, stir, heat till it boils again.
Sweet with honey and season with vanilla and cinnamon. Spread the mixture on dessert bowls and garnish with mint.

9.73 Rhubarb cake with sprinkles

Laxative, antipyretic. Protects the digestive system. Detoxifying, affects anorexia, good to fight flatulence, inflammatory bowel disease, brittle nails and hair. Relieves pain, detoxifying, against dry skin, acne, eczema.
Cooking time approx. 1 1/2 hours
Calories p. portion: 476
8 portions
Allergens: AG

Quantity of ingredients:
Wheat flour 7/8 lbs / 400g. (yes)
Cow's milk (whole milk 3.5% fat) 1 cup / 200g. (little)
Yeast 1 oz / 30g. (yes)
Honey 2 teaspoons / 5g. (yes)
Sunflower oil 2 teaspoons / 5g. (little)
Lemon peel 1 piece / 3g. (yes)
Salt 1 pinch / 1g. (yes)
Rhubarb 2,2 lbs / 800g. (yes)
Margarine 1/4 lbs - 4oz / 120g. (yes)
Wheat flour 3/4 lbs / 300g. (yes)
Vanilla sugar natural 2 pinches / 1g. (yes)
Cinnamon ground 2 pinches / 1g. (yes)
Honey 5 table spoons / 50g. (yes)

Cooking instructions:
Mix flour, grated lemon peel and salt.
Heat milk gently and mix with yeast and honey.
Then add the flour mixture and the oil and knead vigorously. Cover the dough and let it rise in a warm place until it reaches twice the amount. (about 30 minutes)

For the sprinkles, mix flour with vanilla and cinnamon, then add honey and margarine and crumble to a crumbly mass. Keep the sprinkles dough cool.

Lay out a baking sheet with parchment paper.
Knead the dough for the bottom again, roll it out, place it on the baking sheet and let it rise for another 10 minutes.

Clean the rhubarb, wash it, halve lengthwise and cut into pieces of approx. 3 cm. Spread the pieces on the rolled out dough and crumble the sprinkles over the cake.

Place the cake in the preheated oven at 175 ° C and bake for about 40 minutes.

9.74 Rice congee with carrots and fennel

Worms, forcing spleen, relieves constipation, stimulates nerves, detoxifying, reduces inflammation, improves blood circulation, reduces blood pressure, strengthens immune system, prevents cancer, reduces radiation damage.
Cooking time approx. 2 hours and more
Calories p. portion: 131
3 portions
Allergens: G

Quantity of ingredients:
Basic recipe for a rice soup (Congee) 2 cup / 500g. (yes)
Carrot 2 pieces / 100g. (yes)
Fennel 1 piece / 250g. (yes)
Butter organic 1 teaspoon / 3g. (little)
Cardamom 1/2 teaspoon / 1g. (yes)

Cooking instructions:
Cook rice congee according to basic recipe.
Clean and cut carrots and fennel.

When carrots and fennel are cooked from the beginning, they serve wholesomeness. If added shortly before the end of the cooking time, taste and vitamins are retained.

Refine with butter and cardamom before serving.

9.75 Rice congee with dried fruit

Good to fight blood circulation disorders, diarrhea, antipyretic, high blood pressure, a headache, for the drainage of the body overweight and high blood pressure, stops coughing, supports urination. Provides Vitamin C.
Cooking time approx. 10 min
Calories p. portion: 210
2 portions
Allergens: GO

Quantity of ingredients:
Basic recipe for a rice soup (Congee) 4 cups / 500g. (yes)
Butter organic 1/2 teaspoon / 5g. (little)
Apricot dried 6 table spoons / 50g. (yes)
Water 1/2 cup / 50g. (yes)
Maple syrup 1 dash / 3g. (yes)

Cooking instructions:
Cook rice congee according to basic recipe.

Melt a small amount of butter over a low heat and briefly fry small dried fruit with 1/2 cup of water. Add the amount of rice porridge desired for the meal and heat. Serve hot and sweeten with maple syrup if necessary.
Variant: In addition fresh fruit with braise.

9.76 Rice porridge with shrubs (seeds) Yi Yi Ren

Strengths spleen and stomach, strengthens the muscles. Diuretic, supports urination.
Cooking time approx. 25 min
Calories p. portion: 212
2 portions
Allergens:

Quantity of ingredients:
Water 4 cups / 450g. (yes)
Rice variety any 1 cup / 120g. (yes)
Lemon peel 1/4 piece / 2g. (yes)
Coix (seeds) YiYi Ren 1/2 cup / 50g. (yes)
Cress 1 table spoon / 6g. (yes)

Cooking instructions:
Cook rice porridge according to basic recipe with a half cup of Yi Yi Ren and lemon peel. Simmer for 1 hour and then sprinkle cress over it.

9.77 Roasted barley patties

Improves digestion, lowers cholesterol, good to fight diarrhea, ulceration, joint pain, stomach problems. Promotes spleen and liver, reduces blood pressure, strengthens immune system, prevents cancer, reduces radiation damage, stimulates liver function.
Cooking time approx. 1 1/2 hours
Calories p. portion: 398
3 portions
Allergens: ACN

Quantity of ingredients:
Water 1 1/2 cups / 250g. (yes)
Barley grouts 1 cup / 120g. (yes)
Potato 1 piece / 140g. (yes)
Carrot 1 piece / 120g. (yes)
Champignon 2-3 pieces / 25g. (yes)
Chicken egg 1 piece / 55g. (little)
Onion white 1 piece / 50g. (yes)
Ginger fresh 1/2 teaspoon / 1g. (yes)
Pepper (ground) 1 pinch / 0,5g. (yes)
Salt 1 pinch / 1g. (yes)
Lemon 1/2 piece / 15g. (yes)
Parsley 2 table spoons / 15g. (yes)

Peppers powder 1 pinch / 1g. (yes)
Sesame oil 2 table spoons / 50g. (yes)
Bread roll 1 piece / 35g. (little)

Cooking instructions:
Preparation:
Place 2 large cups of hot water in a saucepan; add 1 large cup of barley porridge; simmer for 2 minutes while stirring; then let it swell for 20 minutes on the switched off stove; take down and let cool.

Cook in boiling water 1 large potato, chopped and cut.

Soak 1 roll in hot water and squeeze well.

Then: Mix the barley groats and crushed the potato. Add 1 grated carrot, 2 - 3 chopped mushrooms, 1 egg, 1 finely chopped onion, 1/2 teaspoon grated ginger, a pinch of pepper, a pinch of salt, a little lemon juice, chopped parsley, plenty of rose paprika; knead well and form patties; heat sesame oil in a hot pan; fry the patties for about 15 minutes over a gentle heat; turn at half time.
Also fits well: lettuce, soybean vegetables.

9.78 Rosemary Potatoes

Reduces Inflammation, improves digestion, regenerates skin, supports urination, lowers cholesterol. Rosemary stimulates digestion, strengthens lung, promotes spleen and kidney, dries out.
Cooking time approx. 30 min
Calories p. portion: 188
2 portions
Allergens:

Quantity of ingredients:
Potato 6-8 pieces / 420g. (yes)
Salt (herbal) 1 pinch / 1g. (yes)
Olive oil 1 table spoon / 10g. (yes)
Rosemary 1 teaspoon / 2g. (yes)

Cooking instructions:
Cut the potatoes into half´s, apply a little olive oil on the cut surface, then salt, sprinkle 2 - 3 rosemary needles on the potatoes.
Place the potatoes on the baking tray and bake them in the preheated oven for approx. 25 minutes to 190°C/374°F.

9.79 Rucola salad with tomatoes

Promotes digestion, helps to digest fat, reduces blood pressure, stimulates digestion, helps to fight gastritis, flatulence and heartburn.
Cooking time approx. 10 min
Calories p. portion: 129
1 portions
Allergens: O

Quantity of ingredients:
Olive oil 1 table spoon / 10g. (yes)
Pepper (ground) 1 pinch / 0,2g. (yes)
Salt 1 pinch / 0,3g. (yes)
Vinegar (Apple vinegar) 1 dash / 1g. (yes)
Tomato 4 pieces / 200g. (yes)
Rucola 2 handful / 30g. (yes)

Cooking instructions:
In a salad bowl stir in olive oil, freshly ground pepper, salt, vinegar and diced tomatoes; plenty of finely shredded rucola leaves.
Variants: Cut shiitake mushrooms into fine strips: Fry one half in a little butter and mix with the other half of raw shiitake under the salad. In place of shiitake mushrooms can be used.
Serve with: toasted bread, polenta.

9.80 Russian kasha with white cabbage

Promotes digestion, relieves pain, detoxifying, promotes digestion, stimulates appetite, dissolves stagnation, stimulates blood production and metabolism, reduces fat.
Cooking time approx. 30 min
Calories p. portion: 250
2 portions
Allergens: AG

Quantity of ingredients:
Buckwheat whole grain 1 cup / 130g. (yes)
Water 1 1/2 cups / 240g. (yes)
Nutmeg 1 pinch / 1g. (yes)
Salt 1 pinch / 1g. (yes)
Parsley 1 table spoon / 10g. (yes)
Ground 1 pinch / 2g. (yes)
Butter organic 1 teaspoon / 3g. (little)
White cabbage Handful / 20g. (yes)

Cooking instructions:
Roast buckwheat golden yellow; add boiling water, heat till it boils
briefly and then let it swell until soft; Grate the white cabbage finely and
fold in. Season with nutmeg, a little salt; some parsley, cumin and butter
at the end.

9.81 Salmon on tomato-spinach

Promotes bowel movement, improves blood circulation, reduces
inflammation, improves digestion, regenerates skin, supports urination,
lowers cholesterol, promotes sweating, dissolves stagnation.
Cooking time approx. 1 hour
Calories p. portion: 365
6 portions
Allergens: D

Quantity of ingredients:
Potato 1,1 lbs / 500g. (yes)
Salt 1 pinch / 1g. (yes)
Salmon 1,3 lbs / 600g. (recommended)
Rapeseed oil 2 teaspoons / 24g. (yes)
Tomato 1/4 lbs - 4oz / 100g. (yes)
Spinach 1,5 lbs / 700g. (yes)
Salt 1 pinch / 1g. (yes)
Pine nuts 4 table spoons / 40g. (yes)
Leek 1/4 lbs - 4oz / 120g. (yes)
Olive oil 4 table spoons / 40g. (yes)
Salt 1 pinch / 1g. (yes)
Pepper white (ground) 1 pinch / 0,5g. (yes)

Cooking instructions:
Peel the potato and cut into cubes, cook in salted water.
Cut the salmon into portions and fry slowly and evenly in a frying pan
from both sides, seasoned with salt and pepper, then add the pine nuts
and lightly roast.
Blanch spinach in salted water.
Lightly sweat the finely chopped leek with a little rapeseed oil, add the
blanched spinach and heat evenly.
Just before serving, add the halved cocktail tomatoes to the spinach
and season the vegetables well with salt and pepper.
Arrange the spinach and leek tomato bed with the potatoes, add the
salmon and sprinkle with the salted pine nuts.
Drizzle with a little olive oil and serve the dish.

9.82 Sliced turkey with zucchini

Improves digestion, regenerates skin, supports urination, lowers cholesterol, diuretic. Strengthens blood, strengthens bone marrow. promotes spleen and liver, reduces blood pressure, strengthens immune system.
Cooking time approx. 1 hour
Calories p. portion: 282
6 portions
Allergens: AEGL

Quantity of ingredients:
Turkey breast meat 3/4 lbs / 300g. (yes)
Lemon juice 1 table spoon / 10g. (yes)
Basil 1 teaspoon / 2g. (yes)
Zucchini 1,8 lbs / 800g. (yes)
Corn germ oil 2 table spoons / 20g. (yes)
Basic recipe for a vegetable soup 1/4 lbs - 4oz / 125g. (yes)
Cream, sweet 30% 1/4 lbs - 4oz / 125g. (little)
Soy sauce 1 table spoon / 10g. (yes)
Oat fusion (baby food) 2 table spoons / 16g. (yes)
Potato 1,8 lbs / 800g. (yes)

Cooking instructions:
Cut the turkey meat into thin strips, drizzle with the lemon juice and sprinkle with the basil. Wash and peel the zucchini, removing the stems and flowers. Grate the zucchini coarsely.

Heat 1 tablespoon of oil and fry the turkey meat. Add the vegetable stock and add the cream, put on the lid and simmer for about 10 minutes on low heat. Add the zucchini rasp and the melted flakes. Put the lid back on and steam again for about 10 minutes.

For the baby: Crush about 70 g of potatoes. Put about 150 g of zucchini with meat over it. Chop the meat, mix with the remaining oil.

For the family: Add the sliced meat with the broth, add the soy sauce and cook for another 1-2 minutes. Serve with the potatoes.

9.83 Spelled with fruit and nuts

Stops diarrhea, promotes digestion, appetizing, relieves fatigue, anti-inflammatory (gastrointestinal). Good to fight tumor lesions and leukemia, is antiallergic in food allergies, regulates metabolism, lowers blood glucose and cholesterol.
Cooking time approx. 1 1/2 hours
Calories p. portion: 290
3 portions
Allergens: AH

Quantity of ingredients:
Spelled grain 1 cup / 120g. (yes)
Water 1 cup / 50g. (yes)
Apple (sweet) 1 piece / 220g. (yes)
Apricot 1 piece / 200g. (yes)
Peaches 1 piece / 120g. (yes)
Cinnamon ground 1 pinch / 1g. (yes)
Cardamom 1 pinch / 1g. (yes)
Salt 1 pinch / 1g. (yes)
Strawberries 1 cup / 120g. (yes)
Almond puree 1 table spoon / 15g. (yes)
Cocoa 1 pinch / 1g. (yes)
Walnuts 1 table spoon / 10g. (yes)

Cooking instructions:
Put spelled in hot water and cook.

Then: Give sweet chopped fruit (apples, apricots, peaches) in a little hot water, with a little cinnamon, sauté briefly; ground cardamom and / or coriander, a small pinch of salt, the boiled spelled, berries after season. Put some cocoa and roasted nuts over it.

9.84 Spicy avocado cream with cottage cheese

Anti-inflammatory, good to fight swelling, pain and itching, forcing spleen and digestive system, detoxifying, bactericide.
Cooking time approx. 15 min
Calories p. portion: 614
4 portions
Allergens: G

Quantity of ingredients:
Avocado 2 pieces / 600g. (yes)
Pepper (ground) 1 pinch / 0,5g. (yes)
Salt 1 pinch / 1g. (yes)
Lemon juice 1/2 piece / 15g. (yes)
Peppers powder 1 pinch / 1g. (yes)
Olive oil 1 table spoon / 10g. (yes)
Herbs various 1 table spoon / 7g. (yes)
Cottage cheese 1 cup / 250g. (yes)
Bread with carob kernel flour 8 slices / 200g. (yes)

Cooking instructions:
Peel, core and purée avocados; add plenty of ground pepper, salt, lemon juice, rose paprika, a few drops of oil, chili, fresh chopped herbs, a pinch of salt; cottage cheese (about the same amount as avocado cream), carefully submerge.

Goes well with: Potatoes and millet, with which the avocado cream in combination with vegetable dishes, legumes or lettuce leaves a delicious meal. It is also very good as an appetizer, as a souvenir at parties and as a morning meal in the summer together with a mild dish of lentils or Adzuki beans and grated radish.

9.85 Spicy Tofu Vegetable Pan

Forcing spleen, relieves constipation, detoxifying, reduces inflammation, improves blood circulation, promotes sweating, dissolves stagnation, reduces flatulence, reduces blood pressure, strengthens immune system, prevents cancer, reduces radiation damage.
Cooking time approx. 25 min
Calories p. portion: 241
4 portions
Allergens: EN

Quantity of ingredients:
Sesame oil 2 table spoons / 20g. (yes)
Carrot 2 pieces / 100g. (yes)
Fennel 1 piece / 250g. (yes)
Leek 1 piece / 200g. (yes)
Salt 1 pinch / 1g. (yes)
Turmeric (yellow root) 1 pinch / 1g. (yes)
Lemon juice 1 dach / 1g. (yes)
Soy Tofu 1 package / 120g. (yes)

Pepper (ground) 1 pinch / 0,5g. (yes)
Soy sauce 1 dash / 3g. (yes)
Rice (whole grain) 1 cup / 120g. (yes)
Water 6 cups / 500g. (yes)
Salt 1 pinch / 1g. (yes)

Cooking instructions:
Heat sesame oil in a hot wok or a hot pan; fry the chopped carrots,
fennel and leek slices; salt, a dash of lemon juice, turmeric, tofu cubes
roast for 1 - 2 minutes.
Add the pepper and cook covered for about 5 minutes; drizzle with soy
sauce.
Place the rice in salted water, heat till it boils and let it simmer over low
heat for about 15 minutes.

9.86 Tea Black tea (Russian tea)

Black tea improves blood circulation.
Cooking time approx. 10 min
Calories p. portion: 7
1 portions
Allergens:

Quantity of ingredients:
Black tea 1 table spoon / 5g. (yes)
Water 1 cup / 120g. (yes)

Cooking instructions:
For each cup you use a teaspoonful or a teabag.
Pour green tea only with 60 to 80 ° C / 140 to 176 °F hot water,
otherwise it will be bitter.
If the tea has a stimulating effect, let it draw for two to three minutes. It
has a calming effect for a duration of five minutes (no longer, otherwise
it will be bitter!).
Another method: Pour the tea leaves with about 70 ° C / 158 °F hot
water and pour the water immediately again.
Then just pour hot water again. The bitter substances disappear and
the tea gets a milder aroma.

9.87 Tea from Melissa

Calming effect, good to fight sleep disorders, restlessness and stomach discomfort, allergies, asthma, migraine and bloating, headache, rheumatism. For strengthening after cold and infectious diseases.
Cooking time approx. 10 min
Calories p. portion: 0
4 portions
Allergens:

Quantity of ingredients:
Balm 2 teaspoons / 4g. (yes)
Water 2 cup / 500g. (yes)

Cooking instructions:
Heat the water till it boils and put it aside. Add lemon balm and 10 min. to let go. Sweet to taste with honey. Strain when pouring.

9.88 Tea Green tea

Green tea promotes digestion, supports urination, dissolves mucus, detoxifying, stimulates nerves, reduces blood lipids, lowers cholesterol, reduces inflammation.
Cooking time approx. 10 min
Calories p. portion: 2
1 portions
Allergens:

Quantity of ingredients:
Green tea 1 teaspoon / 2g. (yes)
Water 1 cup / 120g. (yes)

Cooking instructions:
For each cup you use a teaspoonful or a teabag.
Pour green tea only with 60 to 80 ° C / 140 to 176 °F hot water, otherwise it will be bitter.
If the tea has a stimulating effect, let it draw for two to three minutes. It has a calming effect for a duration of five minutes (no longer, otherwise it will be bitter!).
Another method: Pour the tea leaves with about 70 ° C / 158 °F hot water and pour the water immediately again.
Then just pour hot water again. The bitter substances disappear and the tea gets a milder aroma.

9.89 Tofu-Black Bean Chili with Rice

Supports urination, lowers cholesterol, for the drainage of the body overweight and high blood pressure, strengthens immune system.
Cooking time approx. 45 min
Calories p. portion: 344
4 portions
Allergens: AEL

Quantity of ingredients:
Rapeseed oil 1/4 cup / 60g. (yes)
Onion white 2 pieces / 120g. (yes)
Peppers 1 piece / 20g. (yes)
Pepper Cayenne 1 pinch / 0,5g. (yes)
Coriander 1 teaspoon / 2g. (yes)
Thyme 1 teaspoon / 2g. (yes)
Clove 1 teaspoon / 2g. (yes)
Spelled wholemeal flour 2 table spoons / 16g. (yes)
Sherry (whine) 1 table spoon / 8g. (little)
Soy Tofu 5/8 lbs - 8oz / 250g. (yes)
Black beans 2 cans (400g) / 400g. (yes)
Basic recipe for a chicken soup (warming) 1 1/2 cups / 300g. (yes)
Bay leaf 1 piece / 0,2g. (yes)
Garlic 6 pieces / 8g. (yes)
Water 6 cups / 400g. (yes)
Rice Basmati 1 cup / 120g. (yes)

Cooking instructions:
Heat the oil at medium temperature in a large saucepan, add onions, paprika and chili powder and fry for 2 minutes until the onions are glassy.
Add the remaining spices, stirring constantly, stirring until the aroma rises.
Dust the flour, fry for 2 minutes and make sure that the paste-like spice mixture does not burn.
Deglaze with sherry, add the black beans (tin) and mix with the spices.
Add the chicken broth, add the bay leaf and stir in the chopped garlic.
Simmer the beans for 30 minutes and add some chicken stock if needed.
Cook the tofu cubes during the last 10 minutes. The tofu can easily disintegrate and should therefore be lifted very gently with a wooden spoon. Finally, pick out the bay leaf and serve the tofu black bean chili with rice.

9.90 Tomato soup

Promotes digestion, helps to digest fat, supports urination, reduces blood pressure, dissolves stagnation. Contains unsaturated fatty acids, is antioxidativ.
Cooking time approx. 10 min
Calories p. portion: 100
2 portions
Allergens:

Quantity of ingredients:
Olive oil 1 table spoon / 15g. (yes)
Onion white 1 piece / 60g. (yes)
Basil (fresh) 1 teaspoon / 2g. (yes)
Cinnamon ground 1 pinch / 1g. (yes)
Pepper (ground) 1 pinch / 0,5g. (yes)
Salt 1 pinch / 1g. (yes)
Tomato 6 pieces / 250g. (yes)
Water 5/8 lbs - 8oz / 250g. (yes)
Peppers powder 1 pinch / 1g. (yes)

Cooking instructions:
Roast the onion in a pot. Salt and spices. Briefly roast. Put washed and quartered tomatoes in the pan. Stir and sauté briefly. Add a quart of water and heat till it boils. Cook for a quarter of an hour and puree.

9.91 Tsampa with jam or fruit compote

Promotes spleen, diuretic, supports urination, relaxes, stops diarrhea, promotes digestion, appetizing.
Cooking time approx. 5 min
Calories p. portion: 280
1 portions
Allergens: AGO

Quantity of ingredients:
Tsampa (roasted barley flour) 2 table spoons / 30g. (yes)
Water 6-8 table spoons / 70g. (yes)
Butter organic 1/2 teaspoon / 2g. (little)
Strawberry jam 1 table spoon / 7g. (yes)
Sunflower seeds 2 teaspoons / 14g. (yes)
Apple (sweet) 1 piece grated / 120g. (yes)

Cooking instructions:
Pour tsampa with boiling water and stir with a spoon until a porridge is formed.
Add butter, jam, sunflower seeds and grated apple.
Sweet to taste with honey, whole cane sugar, or barley malt.
Spices and herbs: fresh mint, vanilla or cocoa, anise, cinnamon
Summer: jam or compote of your choice
Winter: nuts and apple or pear

9.92 Turkey rolls in tomato cream

Improves digestion, lowers cholesterol, strengthens blood, strengthens bone marrow, good to fight high blood pressure, helps to digest fat, flatulence.
Cooking time approx. 30 min
Calories p. portion: 301
2 portions
Allergens: G

Quantity of ingredients:
Champignon 1/4 lbs - 4oz / 100g. (yes)
Turkey breast meat 5/8 oz / 200g. (yes)
Turkey ham 1/4 lbs - 4oz / 100g. (yes)
Olive oil 2 teaspoons / 6g. (yes)
Tomato 1 piece / 60g. (yes)
Cream, sweet 30% 2 table spoons / 20g. (little)
Garlic 1 piece / 2g. (yes)
Salt 1 pinch / 1g. (yes)
Pepper (ground) 1 pinch / 0,5g. (yes)
Basil (fresh) 1 table spoon / 5g. (yes)
Potato 5/8 oz / 200g. (yes)

Cooking instructions:
Cook potatoes in salted water and peel.
Cut the turkey into schnitzel. Thoroughly clean the mushrooms, rub them and cut them into slices. Spread the mushrooms and boiled ham over the turkey schnitzel. Roll up the schnitzel, fix with a toothpick and fry in oil for about 8-10 minutes from all sides, possibly add some liquid. Briefly dip the meat tomato in boiling water, skin, halve, remove seeds and dice the pulp. Put in the pan. Braise briefly. Add the cream to the turkey rolls and tomato pieces. Heat till it boil.
Season with garlic, salt and pepper. Serve the turkey rolls with the sauce and freshly chopped basil.

9.93 Vegetable bowl with Provencal pistou

Promotes spleen and liver, reduces blood pressure, strengthens immune system, prevents cancer, reduces radiation damage, forcing spleen, dissolves stagnation. Relieves constipation, strengthens mother milk production.
Cooking time approx. 1 1/2 hours
Calories p. portion: 138
8 portions
Allergens: AGL

Quantity of ingredients:
Tomato 5/8 oz / 200g. (yes)
Olive oil 2 table spoons / 30g. (yes)
Garlic 1 clove / 5g. (yes)
Toast bread (whole grain) 1 slice / 5g. (yes)
Parmesan 1 oz / 30g. (little)
Basil (fresh) 1 Bunch / 125g. (yes)
Salt 1 pinch / 2g. (yes)
Pepper (ground) 1 pinch / 1g. (yes)
Oregano dried 1 teaspoon / 3g. (yes)
Basic recipe for a vegetable soup (nutritious) 3 lbs / 1250g. (yes)
Carrot 3/8 lbs - 6oz / 150g. (yes)
Celery root 1/4 lbs - 4oz / 100g. (yes)
Broccoli 5/8 oz / 200g. (recommended)
Fennel 1 piece / 250g. (yes)
Thyme dried 1/2 teaspoon / 2g. (yes)
Oregano dried 1/2 teaspoon / 2g. (yes)
Bay leaf 1 piece / 0,5g. (yes)
Peas, green 1/8 lbs - 2oz / 50g. (yes)
Onion (spring onion) 4 pieces / 80g. (yes)
Potato 1/4 lbs - 4oz / 100g. (yes)

Cooking instructions:
Sauce:
Tear off tomatoes and cut into small pieces. Reduce in a pot with a little olive oil, finely chopped garlic. Add 1 slice of dry toasted bread (crumbed), fresh finely grated Parmesan, finely chopped basil, oregano, salt and pepper.

Soup:
Boil the vegetable broth according to the basic recipe, add coarsely sliced carrots, diced celery, diced potatoes, small florets, broccoli, finely

chopped fennel tuber, peas, thyme, oregano and the bay leaf. let cook 10 minutes.

Cut 4 scallions into thin rings, add them and cook another 2 min.

Pour sauce into a soup bowl. First only a few tablespoons. Stir boiling broth with it, then stir in the soup little by little.

9.94 Vegetable juice

Promotes digestion, helps to digest fat, supports urination, reduces blood pressure, strengthens immune system, prevents cancer, reduces radiation damage, forcing spleen, is stimulating.
Cooking time approx. 15 min
Calories p. portion: 64
1 portions
Allergens: L

Quantity of ingredients:
Celery root 1/2 oz / 20g. (yes)
Carrot 1/4 lbs - 4oz / 100g. (yes)
Tomato 1/4 lbs - 4oz / 100g. (yes)
Garlic 1 piece / 2g. (yes)
Salt 1 teaspoon / 2g. (yes)
Acerola fruit nectar or powder 1/2 teaspoon / 1g. (recommended)

Cooking instructions:
Peel all ingredients and use the juicer to make a drink. Stir in the acerola.

9.95 Vegetable miso soup with tofu

Very powerful, strengthens after febrile illness, reduces blood pressure, strengthens immune system, prevents cancer, reduces radiation damage, improves blood circulation, strengthens liver and kidney, detoxifying, strengthens the muscles, reduces flatulence, forcing spleen.
Cooking time approx. 15 min
Calories p. portion: 107
4 portions
Allergens: EN

Quantity of ingredients:
Sesame oil 2 table spoons / 35g. (yes)
Onion (shallot) 1 piece / 20g. (yes)
Carrot 1 piece / 70g. (yes)
Leek 2 inches / 10g. (yes)
Water 3 cups / 750g. (yes)
Endive salad 2 table spoons / 30g. (yes)
Soy Tofu 2 table spoons / 30g. (yes)
Ginger fresh 1/2 teaspoon / 1g. (yes)
Miso 2 table spoons / 15g. (yes)

Cooking instructions:
In sesame oil first sauté onions, then carrots and a little leek; Pour in water and simmer gently; add the bean sprouts and endive leaves and leave to stand; Tofu cubes, add a little ginger; at the end stir in a little cooled cooking-water the Miso.

9.96 Vegetable semolina soup

Diuretic, harmonizes the stomach and intestines, conducts bowel winds, reduces blood pressure, lowers cholesterol, detoxifying, good to fight loss of appetite, flatulence, inflammatory bowel disease, heartburn, twelffinger intestinal ulcers. Stimulates digestion, reduces pain.
Cooking time approx. 20 min
Calories p. portion: 199
3 portions
Allergens: AEGL

Quantity of ingredients:
Basic recipe for a vegetable soup (nutritious) 2 cup / 500g. (yes)
Potato 1 piece / 80g. (yes)
Parsnip 1 piece / 180g. (yes)
Carrot 1 piece / 120g. (yes)
Celery root 3/8 lbs - 6oz / 150g. (yes)
Kohlrabi 1/2 piece / 200g. (recommended)
Beans (green, fresh) 1/4 lbs / 100g. (recommended)
Wheat semolina 2 table spoons / 24g. (yes)
Lovage 1/2 teaspoon / 2g. (yes)
Butter organic 1 table spoon / 20g. (little)
Soy sauce 1 teaspoon / 3g. (yes)

Cooking instructions:
Worm the prepared vegetable soup; cook the vegetables in the soup softly. Spread some wheatgrass and let it swell. At the end, add lovage-green and a little butter and taste with soy sauce.

9.97 Warming carrot soup

Strengthens and warms, reduces blood pressure, strengthens immune system, prevents cancer, reduces radiation damage, strengthens gastrointestinal function.
Cooking time approx. 30 min
Calories p. portion: 133
3 portions
Allergens: HL

Quantity of ingredients:
Carrot 4 pieces / 250g. (yes)
Walnut oil 2 table spoons / 20g. (yes)
Onion (shallot) 2 pieces / 40g. (yes)
Anise (Common Fennel) 1/2 teaspoon / 1g. (yes)
Nutmeg 1 pinch / 1g. (yes)
Ginger fresh 1/2 teaspoon / 1g. (yes)
Salt 1 pinch / 1g. (yes)
Basic recipe for a vegetable soup (nutritious) 2 cup / 500g. (yes)
Parsley 1 table spoon / 10g. (yes)

Cooking instructions:
Heat walnut oil in a hot pot and fry onions; steam the carrots in it; add anise, nutmeg, a little ginger, salt and sauté everything; add water or vegetable- or meat stock; cook everything soft and then puree; fold in parsley at the end.

Recommendation: Suitable for the cold season, especially if you use meat broth as a liquid for infusion.

9.98 Wheatgrass porridge with pink grapefruit

Little laxative. Promotes digestion. Protects the digestive system. Detoxifying, affects anorexia, good to fight flatulence, inflammatory bowel disease. Warms stomach and spleen.
Cooking time approx. 10 min
Calories p. portion: 398
2 portions
Allergens: AG

Quantity of ingredients:
Cow's milk (1.5% fat) 2 cup / 500g. (yes)
Wheat semolina 1/4 lbs - 4oz / 100g. (yes)
Sugar cane sugar 1/8 lbs - 2oz / 40g. (little)
Grapefruit (Pomelo) 1/2 piece / 120g. (yes)
Sugar cane sugar 2 teaspoons / 4g. (little)
Cinnamon ground 1 pinch / 0,3g. (yes)

Cooking instructions:
Put the milk in a saucepan and heat on the stove. If the milk is warm,
stir in the semolina with a whisk. Add the sugar. Keep it low and wait
until the semolina has absorbed the liquid.

Put in a plate and add chopped crevasses of grapefruit. Sprinkle the
porridge with sugar and cinnamon.

9.99 Whole milk cereal mash

Reduces Inflammation, antiallergic, has a stabilizing effect on the blood
circulation, lowers blood glucose and cholesterol.
Cooking time approx. 20 min
Calories p. portion: 205
1 portions
Allergens: AG

Quantity of ingredients:
Cow's milk (whole milk 3.5% fat) 3/4 cup - 6 oz / 200g. (little)
Water 1/4 cup / 50g. (yes)
Spelled flakes 1/2 oz / 20g. (yes)
Fruit mix juice 1/2 oz / 20g. (yes)

Cooking instructions:
Boil the milk with the wholegrain flakes and let it swell. Add the pureed
fruit.

Switch between wheat, oats and wholemeal spelled flakes, as well as
the fruits. So you get a variety of flavors.

10 Effects of food

10.1 Use ingredients: recommendable

Acai powder
Acerola fruit nectar or powder
Adzuki beans
Amaranth
Amaranth Pops
Beans (green, fresh)
Bitter Herb liqueur
Broccoli
Cauliflower
Cod
Codfish
Cream 10% coffee cream
Fish pieces mixed (fresh water)
Fox nut, gorgon nut, makhana
Fresh cheese from soya
Freshwater fish
Herring
Hibiscus
Kohlrabi

Kudzu
Lentils
Lentils black
Lentils red
Lentils yellow
Lily bulbs
Mascarpone cheese
Mediterranean fish (cod, plaice, haddock, sea eel, mackerel)
Muesli
Perch
Plaice
Rice wild (nature rice)
Rosefish
Salmon
Topinambur
Trout
Turnip
Wheat bran

10.2 Use ingredients: yes

Agar agar (kelp)
Agave nectar
Agrimony
Almond
Almond marzipan
Almond milk
Almond puree
Aloe juice
Anchovy / Sardine
Angelica root
Anise (Common Fennel)
Apple (sour)
Apple (sweet)
Apple juice (natural cloudy)
Apple puree
Apricot
Apricot dried
Apricot jam
Apricot nectar
Apricots
Apricots juice
Arrowroot
Artichoke
Asparagus (green or white)
Aubergine
Avocado

Baking powder
Balm
Bamboo shoots
Banana
Banana (cooking banana)
Banchatee (green tea)
barberry
Barley
Barley flour
Barley grass powder
Barley grouts
Barley malt
Barley not peeled
Basic recipe for a beef soup
Basic recipe for a beef soup (warming)
Basic recipe for a chicken soup (warming)
Basic recipe for a duck soup
Basic recipe for a fish soup
Basic recipe for a rice soup (Congee)
Basic recipe for a vegetable soup (nutritious)
Basil
Basil (fresh)
Batavia
Bay leaf

Bean oil
Bearberry leaf
Beef bone marrow
Beef fillet
Beef lungs (calf)
Beef meat
Beef meat (calf)
Beef meatbones
Berries of the season
Berry juice
Bitter Lemon
Bitter orange peel
Black beans
Black caraway
Black fungus mushroom
Black tea
Blackberry dried (unripe fruit)
Blackberry jam
Blackberry leaves
Blackberry´s
Black-eyed peas
Blackthorn (Sloe)
Blue mallow tee
Blueberry
Blueberry dried
Blueberry jam
Blueberry juice
Bocksdorn fruits (Fructus Lycii, Goji,
goji berry dried
Boletus mushroom
Borage
Borage oil
Boxhorn clover seeds
Brazil nuts
Bread with carob kernel flour
Breadcrumbs (wheat bread, bread roll)
Brie cheese
Broad beans (thick beans)
Brussels sprouts
Buckbean
Buckwheat
Buckwheat (roasted) Kasha
Buckwheat whole grain
Bulgur (cereals)
Burdock root tea
Bush beans
Butter (half fat)
Butter beans white
Buttermilk
Calamari
Cantaloupe
Capers in olive oil
Carambola (Star fruit)
Cardamom

Carob flour, St. john's bread
Carp
Carrot
Carrot (Early Carrot)
Carrot juice without sugar
Cashews
Caviar
Celery root
Celery sticks
Cereal coffee
Chamomile
Chamomile tea
Champignon
Channa-Dal
Chanterelle
Chard
Chenpi (chinese tangerine bowl)
Cherry
Cherry (sour)
Cherry compote
Cherry juice
Chervil
Chervil dried
Chestnut puree
Chestnuts
Chicken Blood
Chicken meat
Chickpeas
Chickweed
Chicory
Chili (pod or ground)
Chinese cabbage
Chinese pearl barley
Chives
Chlorella (fresh water)
Chrysanthemum blossom tea
Cinnamon ground
Cinnamon sticks
Clementine
Clementines
Clove
Cocoa
Coconut flakes
Coconut grated
Coconut meat
Coconut milk
Coffee
Coix (seeds) YiYi Ren
Cola drink
Cola drink (low calorie)
Compote (fruits of the season)
Cooking oil
Coriander
Coriander (fresh)

Corn
Corn (fast polenta)
Corn (roasted)
Corn flour
Corn germ oil
Corn Grease (Polenta)
Corn silk tea
Corn starch
Cottage cheese
Couscous
Cow's milk (1.5% fat)
Crab
Cranberries
Cranberry
Cranberry
Cranberry jam
Cranberry juice
Cream sour 10%
Creamer
Cress
Crispbread
Crucian
Cucumber
Cucumber (bitter)
Cucumber (spicy cucumber)
Cumin (Caraway seed)
Curcuma
Curd cheese 20%
Currant (black)
Currant (red)
Currant (white)
Currant jam (black)
Currant jam (red)
Currant juice (black)
Currants (black)
Currants (red)
Curry
Curry paste red
Daisy
Dandelion (young plants)
Dandelion juice
Dandelionroots tea
Dashi
Dates dried
Dates red
Deer meat
Deer meat
Deer's Bones
Dill
Dulse (seaweed)
Dyer's broom herb
Edam cheese
Elderberries
Elderberry blossom tee

Endive salad
Evening primrose oil
Fennel
Fennel seeds ground
Fennel tea
Fenugreek (Trigonella foenum-graecum)
Fernet Branca (herbal bitter liqueur)
Feta cheese
Fig
Fig dried
Fish innards
Fish remains
Fish sauce
Flounder
Flower pollen
French beans
Fresh cheese
Fresh cheese with herbs
Freshwater crab
Fructose (glucose)
Fruit mix juice
Fruit tea
Gail plum
Galangal
Garam Masala powder
Garlic
Gelatin white
Gelee Royal
Gentian root
Gentian root tea
Ginger fresh
Ginger oil
Ginger powder
Ginkgo fruit
Ginseng
Ginseng root
Goat
Goat and sheep's blood
Goat and sheep's milk
Goat cheese
Goose blood
Gooseberry
Gouda cheese
Gourd
Grape juice red
Grape juice white
Grapefruit (Pomelo)
Grapefruit dried peel
Grapefruit juice
Grapes red
Grapes white
Grapeseed oil
Grass carp

Green spelt
Green tea
Greengage
Ground
Ground caraway
Guava
Halibut (Flatfish)
Hawthorn
Hazelnuts
Herbal tea mix
Herbs bitter
Herbs of Provence
Herbs various
Herbs wild
Hibiscus tea
Hijiki
Hokkaido pumpkin
Honey
Hop
Horehound leaves
Horse meat
Hyssop
Iceberg lettuce
Jasmine blossoms tee
Jellyfish
Juniper berry
Kaki plum
Kalmus
Kefir
Kidney beans (red)
King Solomon's-seal
Kiwi
Kombu seaweed (Saccharina japonica)
Kukicha tea
Kumquats
Lamb bones
Lamb meat
Lamb shoulder
Lamb's lettuce
Lamb's lettuce
Lavender blossoms
Leaf salads (bitter)
Leek
Lemon
Lemon Balm (dried)
Lemon Balm (fresh)
Lemon juice
Lemon peel
Lemongrass
Lettuce
Licorice root tea
Lima beans
Lime
Lime blossom tea

Linseed
Linseed (crushed)
Linseed oil
Liver smoothing tea
Lobster
Longane
Loquate / Japanese medlar
Lotus roots
Lotus seeds
Lovage
Lovage seeds
Luo Han Guo fruit
Lychee
Lychee in Preserved
Lye roll
Mackerel
Mallow (Malva sylvestris) blossom tea
Malt
Mango
Mango juice
Manioc flour
Maple syrup
Mare's milk
Margarine
Margarine (diet)
Marjoram
Medlar
Millet
Millet flakes
Mineral water
Mirabelle plum
Miso
Miso black (fermented)
Miso paste (soy bean paste)
Mixed Pickles
Morel (black, dried)
Morel, dried
Mozzarella
Mu Erh Mushroom
Mulberry fruit
Mulled Wine Spice
Mullet
Multi-grain bread (gray bread)
Mung bean
Mung bean sprouting
Mussels
Mustard
Mustard Dijon
Mustard medium hot
Mustard seeds
Mustard sweet
Mutton
Nasturtium (nose-twister or nose-tweaker)

Nectarine
Nettles
Nori, purple seaweed, red algae
Nutmeg
Oat
Oat flakes (whole grain)
Oat flakes roasted
Oat flour
Oat fusion (baby food)
Oat meal
Oat milk
Octopus
Okra
Olive oil
Olives
Olives green
Onion (shallot)
Onion (spring onion)
Onion read
Onion white
Orange
Orange blossom
Orange dried peel
Orange grated peel
Orange jam
Orange juice
Orange peel
Oregano dried
Oregano fresh
Oyster mushroom
Oyster shell powder
Oysters
Palm oil
Papaya
Parsley
Parsley root
Parsnip
Passion blossoms tea
Passion fruit
Peaches
Peaches (canned)
Peanut oil
Peanuts
Pear
Pear juice
Pearl barley
Pearl barley
Peas
Peas, green
Pepper (ground)
Pepper Cayenne
Pepper powder (hot)
Pepper white (ground)
Peppercorns

Peppermint
Peppermint tea
Pepperoni
Pepperoni, red, pitted, halved
Pepperoni, yellow, pitted, halved
Peppers
Peppers (rose peppers)
Peppers (sweet)
Peppers powder
Pickle
Pig blood
Pigeon
Pimento
Pine nuts
Pineapple
Pineapple (from a can)
Pineapple juice without sugar
Pinto beans speckled
Pistachios
Plum
Plum dried
Plums
Pomegranate
Poppy
Pork lung
Pork meat
Pork skin
Pork's intestine
Potato
Potato (mealy)
Potato flour
Prickly pear
Processed cheese 12%
Psyllium seed
Pudding powder vanilla
Pumpernickel (dark bread)
Pumpkin
Pumpkin seed oil
Pumpkin seeds
Quince
Quinoa
Rabbit
Rabbit (wild)
Rabbit meat
Radicchio
Radish
Radish (white, green, purple-red)
Radish black
Radish horseradish
Radish leaves
Raisins
Rapeseed oil
Raspberry
Raspberry dried (immature)

Raspberry jam
Raspberry leaf tea
Red beet
Red berry (without sugar)
Red cabbage
Reishi mushroom
Rhubarb
Ribworttea
Rice (fragrance)
Rice (Gaoliang / Sorghum)
Rice (whole grain)
Rice Basmati
Rice black
Rice flour
Rice long grain rice
Rice malt
Rice mash
Rice noodles
Rice red
Rice round grain
Rice starch
Rice sticky
Rice sweet
Rice variety any
Romaine lettuce / lettuce salad
Rose blossom tea
Rose hip
Rose hip tea
Rose leaf tea
Rosemary
Rucola
Rusk
Rye
Rye flour
Rye wholemeal bread
Safflower (Dyer's thistle / Hong Hua)
Saffron
Sage
Sago (cereals)
Sake
Salsify
Salt
Salt (herbal)
Sauerkraut (cutted cabbage fermented)
Savory
Savoy cabbage / kale
Sea buckthorn
Sea cucumber
Seacrab
Sesame oil
Sesame oil roasted
Sesame paste (Tahini)
Sesame, black
Sesame, white

Shark
Sheep's milk yoghurt
Shiitake, dried
Shrimp
Shrimps
Skim milk powder
Slug
Sorrel
Sour cherries
Sour milk
Sour milk cheese 20%
Sourdough
Soy flour
Soy noodles
Soy sauce
Soy Tofu
Soy Tofu smoked
Soya Cuisine (soy cream)
Soybean milk
Soybean oil
Soybeans
Soybeans, black
Soybeans, blacks, fermented
Soybeans, yellow
Spelled (Dark) bread
Spelled flakes
Spelled grain
Spelled semolina
Spelled wholemeal flour
Spinach
Spiny lobsters
Spurdog (spiny dogfish, Schillerlocken)
St. Benedict's thistle, blessed thistle,
holy thistle, spotted thistle
Star anise
Stevia (candyleaf, sweetleaf)
Strawberries
Strawberry jam
Strawberry Juice
Sugar fructose - fruit sugar
Sugar glucose - grapes sugar
Sugar Milk Sugar
Sugar substitute (sweetener)
Sunflower seeds
Sweet potato
Tabasco
Tangerine
Tarragon (Estragon)
Tea mixture uric acid lowering
Thistle oil
Thyme
Thyme dried
Toast bread (whole grain)
Tomato

Tomato dried
Tomato juice
Tomato paste
Tomato puree
Tonic Water
Trout (smoked)
Truffle
Tsampa (roasted barley flour)
Tuna
Turkey breast meat
Turkey ham
Turmeric (yellow root)
Turnips
Umeboshi paste
Umeboshi plums (Japanese apricots)
Valerian
Vanilla
Vanilla pod
Vanilla powder
Vanilla sugar natural
Vegetable juice
Vinegar (Apple vinegar)
Vinegar (Red wine vinegar)
Vinegar Aceto Balsamico
Vinegar Aceto Balsamico white
Wakame
Walnut oil
Walnuts
Water
Water hot
Watermelon
Wax gourd

Wheat
Wheat bulgur
Wheat flakes
Wheat flour
Wheat flour whole grain
Wheat germ oil
Wheat semolina
Wheat semolina for children
Wheat/Rye/Gray-black bread with yeast
Wheatgrass juice
Wheatgrass powder
Whey
White beans
White cabbage
Whitefish
Whole grain bread
Wholemeal flour
Wild boar meat
Wild garlic (garlic spinach)
Wild herbs
Wild strawberries
Wormwood herb
Yam root, yam root tuber
Yarrow
Yarrow tea
Yeast
Yew nut
Yoghurt vanilla
Yogi tea
Yogurt (natural, 1.5% fat)
Zucchini

10.3 Use ingredients: little

Beef heart
Beef heart (calf)
Beef kidney
Beef liver
Beef Oxtail pieces
Beef soup meat
Beef stomach
Beer (alcohol-free)
Beer (alcohol-reduced)
Beer (Pils)
Beer (Top-fermented German dark beer)
Bitter liqueur
Bread roll
Brown ale
Butter organic
Camembert
Campari

Chicken egg
Chicken egg white
Chicken heart
Chicken liver
Chicken stomach
Chocolate
Chocolate (Diabetic)
Clarified butter
Coconut fat
Cow's milk (whole milk 3.5% fat)
Cream (30% fat)
Cream sour 20%
Cream sour 30%
Cream, sweet 30%
Créme fraiche cheese
Curd cheese 40%
Deer's kidneys
Duck (heart)

Duck (slaughtered)
Ducks egg
Eel
Eel smoked
Emmental cheese
Feta cheese
Ginseng liqueur
Goat and sheep's brain
Goat and sheep's liver
Goat and sheep's stomach
Goose
Goose egg
Goose fat
Goose parts
Gorgonzola
Honey wine (Met)
Ladyfingers
Lamb kidneys
Lamb liver
Lychee liqueur
Martini
Mayonnaise 50%
Mayonnaise 80%
Mold cheese
Mutton
Noodles (wheat) with egg
Noodles (wheat, lasagne) with egg
Noodles (wheat, ribbon noodles) with egg
Noodles (wheat, spaghetti) with egg
Noodles (whole grain) with egg
Octopus
Parmesan
Peanut (roasted)
Peanut butter
Pheasant
Pigeon egg
Pork Bacon
Pork brain
Pork fat (lard)
Pork ham
Pork ham cooked

Pork ham smoked
Pork heart
Pork kidneys
Pork knuckle
Pork liver
Pork marrow bones
Pork sausage (Bratwurst)
Pork stomach
Pork/beef sausage (smoked)
processed cheese 30%
Prosecco
Puff pastry
Quail
Quail egg
Rabbit liver
Red wine
Rum
Sheep's milk
Sherry (whine)
Sour cream 15% fat
Spirit
Sugar - icing sugar
Sugar brown
Sugar candy white
Sugar cane sugar
Sugar molasses
Sugar palm sugar
Sugar white
Sunflower oil
Walnuts roasted
Wheat beer
Wheat flatbread/pita bread
White bread (baguette)
White bread (pretzel sticks)
White bread (roll)
White bread (wheat bread)
White breadcrumbs
White dumpling bread (wheat bread cut into chunks)
White wine
Wormwood
Yogurt (natural, 3.5% fat)

10.4 Do not use contra-acting foods

Chicken yolk
Pork Lard

Supplementary nutrition

11 Herbs and their effects

11.1 Basil

It has a beneficial effect on flatulence and nausea, relaxing and soothing. Good to fight emphysema, bronchitis, whooping cough, high blood pressure, headache, mouth odor, warts, hiccup, gout, migraine.

11.2 Dill

The medicinal and spice herb has an antispasmodic effect and stimulates gastric juice production. Good to fight flatulence. Antispasmodic for gastrointestinal discomfort.

11.3 Chervil dried

Forces urination, detoxifying, blood-purifying and blood-pressure-reducing effects.

11.4 Coriander

The essential oils are appetizing, digestive, cramping and soothing in stomach and intestinal disorders.

11.5 Herbs various

Appetizing, lots of trace elements and vitamins

11.6 Cress

Diuretic, supports urination. Good to fight dry mouth, inner agitation, sore throat, diabetes, kidney stones, gastrointestinal complaints, lung problems, menstrual cramps or cancer.

11.7 Chives

Bactericide, prevents cancer, strengthens gastric juice production, promotes digestion and blood circulation, promotes growth, triggers stagnation.

11.8 Lovage

Stimulates digestion, reduces pain. Extracts of the root are used to flush out urinary tract infections and prevent kidney gravel.

11.9 Lily bulbs

Calms nerves, good to fight scaly skin. The onions and the petals are added to ointments in the Orient, which can heal muscles and tendons. White lily (astringent).

11.10 Dandelion (young plants)

Detoxifies, relieves inflammation. Regulates digestion, helps with rheumatism, releases kidney stones, leaves pimples and chronic skin disorders disappear.

11.11 Balm

Soothing effect, Good for insomnia, restlessness and upset stomach, Allergies, Asthma, Migraine, Flatulence, Headache, Rheumatism and mental tension. To strengthen after cold and infectious diseases.

11.12 Oregano dried

It has an anti-digestive, calming and nerve-strengthening effect, helps to fight cramping stomach and intestinal disorders. The ingredient Carvacrol has an anti-inflammatory effect.

11.13 Parsley

Stimulates liver function, detoxifies. Forces urinating. Relieves flatulence. Digestive and menstrual stimulating, birth-accelerating, memory-enhancing, blood-purifying, skin-smoothing.

11.14 Peppermint

Relaxes, frees the lungs and the nose (inhale), regulates the cycle. Stimulates bile flow and bile production, antispasmodic in gastrointestinal disorders, antimicrobial and antiviral.

11.15 Rosemary

Promotes digestion, relieves bloating, strengthens lung, spleen and kidney. Affects the circulation and nerves. Appetizing. Baths help to fight circulatory disorders as well as with gout and rheumatism.

11.16 Sage

Good to fight yeast infections. The leaves have a digestive effect and are used in greasy foods. Antiperspirant effect. Helps to relieve coughing attacks. Dries out (TCM).

11.17   Black caraway

Detoxifying, immunoregulatory. In addition, the oil should stimulate the formation of bone marrow cells and generally protect body cells from viruses.

11.18   Thyme dried

Disinfecting. It stimulates the blood circulation, increases the appetite and helps to digest fat meat better. Strengthens lungs and spleen (TCM).

11.19   King Solomon's-seal

Used to repair wounds or damaged tissue. Good to fight dry cough, earlier also tuberculosis and dysentery, as well as diarrhea and hemorrhoids.

11.20   Yam root, yam root tuber

Solves cramps (in the gastrointestinal tract). Digestive through increased bile production. Anti-inflammatory in rheumatic diseases.
Mucolytic agent for coughing. Relief of menopausal symptoms.

12 Basics of Nutrition

The basic principles of nutrition described herein are general recommendations. They are not aimed at a specific form of therapy. Recommendations concerning a therapy have priority.

12.1 Nutrition

Regular meals in a relaxed atmosphere. A warm breakfast is considered a good start into the day.

The main meals ought to be taken for lunch – supper in the early evening. Pay attention to feeling hungry or sated: don't eat too much nor remain hungry is the rule

Prepare the meals freshly from natural, regional products. Frozen, heat-conserved, industrially prepared or foodstuffs cooked in the microwave oven are rejected.

Choice of foodstuffs according to the season: more cooling food in summer, more warming food in winter.

Eat cooked food at least twice a day. Food and drinks ought to be lukewarm, never ice-cold or hot.

Raw vegetables, briefly cooked vegetables, freshly squeezed juices and mineral water are not recommended. Milk and dairy products are only included in the diet if they don't cause problems.

Don't use therapeutic recipes over a longer period without consulting your doctor or therapist.

Varied food
Enjoy the diversity of foodstuffs. Characteristics of a balanced nutrition are variety, suitable combination and a balanced quantity of rich and low energy foodstuffs (on one hand avoiding undersupply with essential nutrients and on the other hand to take to many undesirable substances).

A lot of Cereal Products - and Potatoes
Bread, pasta, rice, cereal flakes (best wholemeal) as well as potatoes contain almost no fat, but many vitamins, mineral nutrients, trace elements, roughage and secondary plant substances. These foodstuffs ought to be taken with low-fat side dishes.

Vegetables and Fruit – „Take Five" every day ...
5 portions of vegetables and fruit a day, as fresh as possible, briefly cooked, or maybe one portion as a juice – ideal as a side dish to every meal as well as snack between meals: Thus a lot of vitamins, mineral nutrients as well as roughage and secondary plant substances

Daily milk and dairy products
Milk and Dairy Products every Day, once or twice per Week Fish; meat, sausages as well as eggs moderately. These foodstuffs contain valuable nutrients like calcium in the milk, iodine selenium and omega-3 fat acids in saltwater fish. Meat is favorable due to its high content of disposable iron and the vitamins B1, B6 and B12. Quantities of 300 – 600 g meat and sausage per week are sufficient. Prefer low-fat products, especially in meat- and dairy products.

Low-fat and fatty Foodstuffs
Fat supplies us with essential fat acids and fatty foodstuffs contain also fat-soluble vitamins. Fat is high in energy; therefore much fat in the food may cause overweight, possibly also cancer. Too many saturated fat acids may further a tendency for cardio-vascular diseases in the long term. Prefer vegetable oils and fats (e.g. rapeseed-, olive-, soya-oils and solid fats produced therefrom). Beware of invisible fat in meat- and dairy products, pastry and sweets as well as in fast-food and convenience foods. 70 – 90 g fat per day is sufficient.

Moderately Sugar and Salt
Take sugar and foods/drinks containing various kinds of sugar (e.g. glucose syrup) only occasionally. Use herbs and spices as well as a little salt creatively. Prefer salt containing iodine.

Plenty of Liquids
Water is absolutely essential. Drink 1-2 l liquids every day. Prefer water (with or without gas) and other low-calorie drinks. Alcoholic drinks should not be taken.

Tasty Dishes, carefully cooked
Cook the meals with as low temperatures and as short as possible, using little water and fat – this preserves the original taste, keeps the nutrients intact and prevents the production of harmful compounds.

Take time and enjoy the food
Take your Time and enjoy your Food
Eating consciously helps to eat right. The eye enjoys food, too. It's fun, invites to enjoy varied dishes and stimulates the feeling of satiety.

Watch your Weight and stay in Motion
A balanced diet and a lot of exercise and sport (30 – 60 min/day) are a healthy combination. The right weight furthers well-being and health. Thermals, directional effectiveness, digestive power

There are various criteria for judging the effectiveness of herbs and foodstuffs.

The use of certain herbs and ingredients is based on observations of the effects on the body which these foodstuffs, herbs and spices show after having eaten them. The medical science has developed following system: Every ingredient or herb has a directional effectiveness. Furthermore, there are herbs which have a special effect on certain organs.

The basic condition for a healthy metabolism is to obtain sufficient energy from food and that the digestive process doesn't use too much energy. An easily digestible meal makes content and sated, doesn't cause flatulence and fatigue after the meal. The perfect spices increase the healthiness of our meals. Very often, just small doses of herbs and spices will suffice. They are not used to make us sated, but to help our digestive organs to digest the food.

12.2 Recipes

The recipes list the ingredients to be used and the cooking instructions show how the dish is prepared. The list of ingredients shows the concerned quantities as well as the relevance for the therapy. If you find „less than mentioned", try to comply or find an alternative from the „list of recommended foodstuffs". Mostly it shall result just in a small change of taste when you simply avoid this ingredient.

Mild cooking methods: boiling, stewing, poaching, steaming
Strong cooking methods: barbecuing, roasting, frying, smoking
Balanced cooking methods: deep-frying, baking brick
Deep-freezing and warming in the microwave oven should be avoided (denaturalization).

12.3 Foodstuffs

Foodstuffs have an effect on body and soul like medicinal herbs, only a very much milder one. Dietary advice is mainly based on regional foodstuffs. The knowledge about the effects of each foodstuff and the knowledge, when which foodstuff shall be used, is based on the orthodoschool of medicine. Use ecologic-organic products, if possible. As everything should be cooked for a long time due to a better digestability and very rarely eaten raw, the food agrees with everyone.

The classification of the foodstuffs according to their effect on the body is the basis in order to achieve a harmonious status of health.

Dietary advisors do not recommend certain foodstuffs for everyone. The individual diet is tailor-made for the individual constitution.

Buy only fresh and ripe fruit and vegetables. You ought to leave unripe fruit and vegetables and such with brown spots and wilted leaves behind in the market. In this case take deep-frozen goods (never ready-to-serve dishes!). Fruit and vegetables are deep-frozen immediately after harvesting and often contain more vitamins and minerals than the goods from the vegetable shelf. Whereas conserved or tinned goods contain very much less biological substances. Also, salt, sugar and others are mostly added to the latter. Never leave the foodstuffs in the water after washing them to avoid that many vital substances get drowned. Clean salads, fruit and vegetables immediately before serving.

Please make sure of the hygienic processing of foodstuffs. Clean your salads, fruit and vegetables carefully. When cooking with meat, prepare all ingredients first and then process the meat products. Clean the worktop and tools very carefully. Wooden surfaces ought to be treated with a mild disinfectant regularly in order to reduce germination.

Store fruit and vegetables separately, if possible. Harvested fruit and vegetables are still alive and emit e.g. ethylene gas, which makes other products ripen and age faster. Keep meat and fish in the closed packaging or store them in the fridge in closed containers.

12.4 Herbs

There are some basic rules for storing medicinal herbs. On principle, herbs must be protected from direct sunlight, humidity and heat.

Containers for the storage of herbs may be glasses, ceramic jars and even plastic containers. However, plastic is a rather unsuitable material and should only be a short-term solution. In case of glass containers, use a dark material.

Medicinal herbs cannot be kept for any long period. The shelf life of herbs is limited. However, it can be prolonged with suitable storage. The place should be dark, rather cool and absolutely dry. A wooden medicine cabinet, placed not directly next to a source of heat, would be ideal. Never buy large quantities of herbs so as not to have to throw them away. Label the container with the name of the herb and the date of harvesting or processing.

13 Other dietic-books

The following syndromes of dietetics, TCM or for a therapy supplement for cancer are available.

Dietetics

E001. Nutrition of the infant - baby food
E002. Nutrition during lactation
E003. Nutrition in old age
E004. Nutrition of children and adolescents
E005. Nutrition of athletes
E006. Light weight
E007. Pregnancy
E008. Full food

Protein and electrolyte - kidneys
E009. (hemodialysis) dialysis treatment
E010. Acute renal failure
E011. Chronic renal insufficiency
E012. Nephrotic syndrome
E013. Kidney stones (nephrolithiasis)

Gastrointestinal tract - pancreas
E014. Acute pancreatitis (inflammation of the pancreas)
E015. Chronic pancreatitis (inflammation of the pancreas)

Gastrointestinal tract - small intestine and large intestine
E016. Acute obstipation (constipation)
E017. Chronic obstipation (constipation)
E018. Colon irritabile
E019. Diverticulitis
E020. Acquired lactose intolerance (lactose malabsorption)
E021. Fructose malabsorption
E022. Glutensensitive enteropathy (celiac disease)
E023. Colectomy
E024. Short Bowel Syndrome

Gastrointestinal tract - liver, gallbladder, bile ducts
E025. Acute and chronic hepatitis (inflammation of the liver)
E026. Cholelithiasis (bile stones)
E027. fatty liver
E028. cirrhosis

Gastrointestinal tract - Stomach and duodenal intestine
E029. Acute gastritis
E030. Chronic gastritis
E031. Stomach bleeding
E032. Ulcus ventriculi and duodenal ulcer
E033. Condition after gastric surgery

Gastrointestinal tract - oral cavity and esophagus
E034. Stomatitis
E035. Esophageal carcinoma (esophageal cancer)
E036. Refluosophagitis (heartburn)

Special diseases
E037. Phenylketonuria (PKU)
E038. Rheumatic joint diseases

Metabolism
E039. Obesity (overweight)
E040. Diabetes mellitus
E041. Eating disorders (underweight)

Fat metabolism
E042. Hypercholesterolaemia (increased cholesterol level)
E043. Hepatic Encephalopathy

Heart and circulation
E044. Arteriosclerosis (arterial calcification)
E045. Heart insufficiency
E046. Hypertension
E047. Hyperuricaemia and gout

Changed nutrient requirements
E048. In case of fever
E049. For malignant diseases
E050. After burns
E051. Radiation and chemotherapy

CANCER
E100. Pancreatic cancer
E101. Bladder cancer
E102. Blood cancer (leukemia)
E103. Breast cancer
E104. Colorectal cancer
E105. Gastric cancer
E106. Kidney cancer
E107. Esophageal cancer

TCM
E200. Bladder - moisture heat in the bladder
E201. Bladder - moisture and cold in the bladder
E202. Bladder - emptiness and cold in the bladder
E203. Large intestine - external cold affects the large intestine
E204. Large intestine - moisture heat in the large intestine
E205. Large intestine - heat blocks the intestine II acute
E206. Large intestine - dryness of the colon
E207. Large intestine - Yang deficiency (cold)
E208. Heart - Blood insufficiency
E209. Heart - Blood stagnation
E210. Heart - Fire
E211. Heart - Hot mucus clogs the heart pores

E212. Heart - Cold mucus clogs the heart pores
E213. Heart - Qi deficiency
E214. Heart - Yang deficiency
E215. Heart - Yin deficiency
E216. Liver - Ascending Liver Yang
E217. Liver - Blood deficiency
E218. Liver - Blood stagnation
E219. Liver - Moisture heat in liver and gall bladder
E220. Liver - Fire
E221. Liver - Gall bladder Qi-Empty
E222. Liver - Cold in the liver meridian
E223. Liver - Qi stagnation
E224. Liver - Wind
E225. Liver - Wind with ascending liver Yang
E226. Liver - Wind with blood anemic
E227. Liver - Wind with extreme heat
E228. Lung - Qi deficiency
E229. Lung - Mucus-moisture in the lungs
E230. Lung - Mucus-heat in the lungs
E231. Lung - Mucus-cold in the lungs
E232. Lung - Dryness of the lungs
E233. Lung - Wind-heat attacks the lungs
E234. Lung - Wind-cold affects the lungs
E235. Lung - Yin deficiency
E236. Stomach - Bloodstagnation
E237. Stomach - Fire
E238. Stomach - Cold with liquid
E239. Stomach - Nutrition stagnation
E240. Stomach - Qi deficiency
E241. Stomach - Rebellious Qi
E242. Stomach - Yin Emptiness
E243. Spleen - Heat and moisture attack the spleen
E244. Spleen - Coldness and moisture affects the spleen
E245. Spleen - Qi deficiency
E246. Spleen - Qi deficiency + Declining spleen Qi
E247. Spleen - Qi deficiency + spleen does not control the blood
E248. Spleen - Yang deficiency
E249. Kidney - Heart and kidney no longer communicate
E250. Kidney - Jing deficiency
E251. Kidney - Kidneys cannot receive the Qi
E252. Kidney - Qi is not stable
E253. Kidney - Yang deficiency
E254. Kidney - Yin deficiency

For further information visit di-book.com.